MIDLOTHIAN
PUBLIC LIBRARY

READINGS ON

HERMAN MELVILLE

Other titles in the Greenhaven Press
Literary Companion Series:

American Authors

Nathaniel Hawthorne
Ernest Hemingway
Arthur Miller
John Steinbeck
Mark Twain

British Authors

Jane Austen

World Authors

Sophocles

British Literature

The Canterbury Tales
Shakespeare: The Comedies
Shakespeare: The Sonnets
Shakespeare: The Tragedies

THE GREENHAVEN PRESS
Literary Companion
TO AMERICAN AUTHORS

HERMAN MELVILLE

David Bender, *Publisher*
Bruno Leone, *Executive Editor*
Scott Barbour, *Managing Editor*
Bonnie Szumski, *Series Editor, Book Editor*

Greenhaven Press, San Diego, CA

Library of Congress Cataloging-in-Publication Data

Readings on Herman Melville / Bonnie Szumski, book editor.
          p.   cm. — (The Greenhaven Press literary com-
panion to American authors)
     Includes bibliographical references and index.
     ISBN 1-56510-584-2 (lib. bdg. : alk. paper). —
ISBN 1-56510-583-4 (pbk. : alk. paper)
     1. Melville, Herman, 1819–1891—Criticism and inter-
pretation. I. Szumski, Bonnie, 1958–   . II. Series.
PS2387.R37   1997
813'.3—dc20   96-20863
                                                       CIP

Copyright ©1997 by Greenhaven Press, Inc.
PO Box 289009
San Diego, CA 92198-9009
Printed in the U.S.A.

66 *What I feel most moved to write, that is banned,— it will not pay. Yet, altogether, write the* other *way I cannot. So the product is a final hash, and all my books are botches.* *99*

Herman Melville, from a letter to Nathaniel Hawthorne, despairing of his lack of success or acceptance

CONTENTS

took that ghastly, bloody, dramatic conflict to inspire some of his greatest poetry. From this point on, Melville's poetry was both more complex and more beautiful.

Chapter 2: A Critical Selection

Chapter 3: *Moby Dick*

Hinduism that clearly influenced the work, especially in the sections that compare the Judeo-Christian and pagan traditions.

Chapter 4: *Billy Budd*

FOREWORD

*"'Tis the good reader that
makes the good book."*
Ralph Waldo Emerson

The story's bare facts are simple: The captain, an old and
scarred seafarer, walks with a peg leg made of whale ivory.
He relentlessly drives his crew to hunt the world's oceans for
the great white whale that crippled him. After a long search,
the ship encounters the whale and a fierce battle ensues. Finally the captain drives his harpoon into the whale, but the
harpoon line catches the captain about the neck and drags
him to his death.

A simple story, a straightforward plot—yet, since the 1851
publication of Herman Melville's *Moby Dick*, readers and
critics have found many meanings in the struggle between
Captain Ahab and the whale. To some, the novel is a cau-
tionary tale that depicts how Ahab's obsession with revenge
leads to his insanity and death. Others believe that the whale
represents the unknowable secrets of the universe and that
Ahab is a tragic hero who dares to challenge fate by attempting to discover this knowledge. Perhaps Melville intended Ahab as a criticism of Americans' tendency to become involved in well-intentioned but irrational causes. Or
did Melville model Ahab after himself, letting his fictional
character express his anger at what he perceived as a cruel
and distant god?

Although literary critics disagree over the meaning of
Moby Dick, readers do not need to choose one particular interpretation in order to gain an understanding of Melville's
novel. Instead, by examining various analyses, they can gain

numerous insights into the issues that lie under the surface of the basic plot. Studying the writings of literary critics can also aid readers in making their own assessments of *Moby Dick* and other literary works and in developing analytical thinking skills.

The Greenhaven Literary Companion Series was created with these goals in mind. Designed for young adults, this unique anthology series provides an engaging and comprehensive introduction to literary analysis and criticism. The essays included in the Literary Companion Series are chosen for their accessibility to a young adult audience and are expertly edited in consideration of both the reading and comprehension levels of this audience. In addition, each essay is introduced by a concise summation that presents the contributing writer's main themes and insights. Every anthology in the Literary Companion Series contains a varied selection of critical essays that cover a wide time span and express diverse views. Wherever possible, primary sources are represented through excerpts from authors' notebooks, letters, and journals and through contemporary criticism.

Each title in the Literary Companion Series pays careful consideration to the historical context of the particular author or literary work. In-depth biographies and detailed chronologies reveal important aspects of authors' lives and emphasize the historical events and social milieu that influenced their writings. To facilitate further research, every anthology includes primary and secondary source bibliographies of articles and/or books selected for their suitability for young adults. These engaging features make the Greenhaven Literary Companion series ideal for introducing students to literary analysis in the classroom or as a library resource for young adults researching the world's great authors and literature.

Exceptional in its focus on young adults, the Greenhaven Literary Companion Series strives to present literary criticism in a compelling and accessible format. Every title in the series is intended to spark readers' interest in leading American and world authors, to help them broaden their understanding of literature, and to encourage them to formulate their own analyses of the literary works that they read. It is the editors' hope that young adult readers will find these anthologies to be true companions in their study of literature.

INTRODUCTION

This volume in the Greenhaven Press *Literary Companion Series* illuminates the work of novelist and poet Herman Melville. Although Melville's works may seem overly wordy and philosophically heavy to many readers today (as indeed they did to readers in his own time), there are few more satisfying endeavors than discovering Melville's peculiar blend of humor and depth. Although best known for his novel *Moby Dick*, to which volumes of analysis have been devoted, Melville's other works are just as deeply satisfying, as is his poetry.

A reader approaching Melville today perhaps will need more patience than ever to delve deeply into his work. A lover of words and the timeless themes that have intrigued all truly great writers, Melville demands much of his readers. He expects a tolerable understanding of Western and Eastern religious philosophy, a knowledge of the great Western philosophers, and a desire to explore uniquely human qualities: the capacities to think, question, and ponder our place in the world. This pursuit may seem less intriguing, perhaps, in an age when many writers spoonfeed us, rarely referring to the immense religious and philosophical tradition that Herman Melville demands we acknowledge. Yet those who decide to pursue Melville will be participating in the thoughts of one of our greatest religious thinkers, as profound a theologian as any called by such a name.

Readings on Herman Melville helps the reader gather information and gain insight into what Melville cared about and why. Essays cover and clarify the themes that intrigued Melville and the way in which these themes were vital to his work. Chosen for their readability, essays both point out to readers the breadth of Melville's talents and place him in a historical context.

Each volume in the *Literary Companion Series* includes helpful features for those new to literary criticism. Each essay's introduction summarizes the article's main ideas and gives a bit of background on the author. Notes explain difficult or unfamiliar words and concepts throughout the book. A chronology lists important dates in the life of the author and presents him in a broader historical context. A bibliography includes works for further research as well as historical works of interest. Finally, a detailed table of contents and thorough index make each volume in the *Literary Companion Series* a complete research tool in itself as well as a launching point for further exploration.

While examining the work of Herman Melville, or any author who demands the best of us as readers, it may be useful to remember what the author himself, in his usual half-mocking, half-serious way, said of pursuing the depths of the intellect and the soul:

> It is a frightful poetical creed that the cultivation of the brain eats out the heart. But it's my *prose* opinion that in most cases, in those men who have fine brains and work them well, the heart extends down to hams. And though you smoke them with the fire of tribulation, yet, like veritable hams, the head only gives the richer and the better flavour. I stand for the heart.

HERMAN MELVILLE: A BIOGRAPHY

During his lifetime, Herman Melville was acknowledged as a great writer only for his early adventure novels, *Typee* and *Omoo*. Like fans who typecast an actor, the public would not accept the later work that Melville believed to be his true destiny. As Melville's work became more obscure, more deep, and more demanding, the few readers who had retained any loyalty abandoned him. He found little support in family members who were similarly puzzled by his work. Even *Moby Dick*, Melville's best-known novel, received accolades in some publications as a realistic sea adventure but was panned for its more philosophical insights. Melville, of course, was more interested in the philosophical insights, and refused to write what he termed "the other way." He wanted to join the "corps of thought-divers, that have been diving and coming up again with bloodshot eyes since the world began." The struggle to maintain a belief in his work in the face of strong public resistance often left him alternately depressed and raging. Melville's almost contemptuous lack of respect for his reading public and simultaneous desire for public appreciation dogged his career.

Herman Melvill was born on August 1, 1819, in New York City. (The family would add the final *e* much later.) He was the third child of Allan Melvill and Maria Gansevoort Melvill. The Melville family would eventually consist of eight children, four boys and four girls, of whom Melville was the second son. Both Herman's father and mother came from distinguished American families. Major Thomas Melvill, Herman's paternal grandfather, had been a Mohawk at the Boston Tea Party and was appointed Collector of Port of Boston by President Washington in 1789. Herman's maternal grandfather, General Peter Gansevoort, had prevented the British from reinforcing General Burgoyne before the

Battle of Saratoga during the American Revolution.

With his father a world traveler and both his grandfathers Revolutionary War heroes, Melville grew up hearing tales of adventure. As a boy, Herman was especially intrigued by the mementos and souvenirs from distant lands that filled his home. His family owned several pieces of furniture from Europe that became objects of his contemplation. He later wrote: "These [pieces] I examined again and again, wondering where the wood grew: whether the workmen who made them still survived, and what they could be doing with themselves now." He seemed, from a young age, preoccupied with travel.

Melville's father, an importer of French goods, was a wealthy businessman whose success in Herman's early childhood enabled him to move his growing family to more and more expensive homes in New York. But Allan Melvill's business was always unpredictable, and when in 1830 the American economy took an unfortunate downturn, Melvill's business suffered greatly. The family was forced to move nearer to Maria's parents in Albany. There, unable to rescue his business from debt, Allan Melvill died two years later, when Herman was twelve years old.

GROWING BITTER BEFORE HIS TIME

Allan Melvill's death left his family in poverty. Since women of Maria Gansevoort's social stature did not do paid work, she and her family were supported by her brothers. The Melville boys were taken out of school and put to work. Herman was placed as a bank clerk and his seventeen-year-old brother Gansevoort was hired into the family's fur business. Melville would never again attend school regularly, though he would fit in several semesters of schooling over the next five years whenever he was able to take time away from the need to make money for his family. Melville recalled the crushing weight of responsibility placed upon him for the family's well-being years later in a letter chastising a friend:

> Talk not of the bitterness of middle age and afterlife . . . a boy can feel all that, and much more, when upon his young soul the mildew has fallen. . . . Before the death of my father I never thought of working for my living, and never knew there were hard hearts in the world. . . . I had learned to think much, and bitterly, before my time.

Herman alternated between jobs at the bank and the fur

business while his mother and other siblings spent winters in Albany and summers in Pittsfield, Massachusetts, on the farm of Thomas Melville, Herman's uncle. In 1837 a financial panic put Gansevoort out of business. Seeking to reduce expenses, Maria Melville moved to Lansingburgh, New York, in November 1838. Herman tried to help the family financially by teaching at various schools, but found the work unrewarding, boring, and poorly paid. In May 1839, Melville published his first known fiction, "Fragments from a Writing Desk," in a Lansingburgh newspaper.

FIRST VOYAGE

Soon after, unable to find consistent work in what was then a serious economic depression, Herman decided to attempt his first voyage to Liverpool and back. Herman's cousin Leonard Gansevoort had just come back from a four-year whaling cruise, and his tales were so exciting that Herman decided to try his hand at working on a ship. So on Monday morning, June 5, Melville signed on as "boy," or low-ranking hand, on a merchant ship, the *St. Lawrence.* On his return later that year, Herman found his mother in even more desperate straits than on his departure. Mortgages on her property were being foreclosed and she was auctioning off her furniture. Herman responded to her plight by taking several teaching jobs, which paid little to nothing and which convinced him that teaching was a hopeless career. He then visited his uncle Thomas Melvill in Galena, Illinois, hoping to find work out west. When no work materialized, he returned to New York in the fall of 1840.

LATER VOYAGES

Frustrated by his lack of employment, Melville decided to try his hand at whaling, leaving for Nantucket near Christmas of 1840. There he joined the crew of the *Acushnet,* a new two-masted whaling vessel. The *Acushnet* sailed on January 5, 1841. Hunting whales in the South Atlantic, it then rounded Cape Horn, cruised the Galapagos Islands region and sailed to the Marquesas Islands—where Melville deserted.

Melville had grown to hate the *Acushnet*'s tyrannical captain, who neglected and starved his crew. He and companion Toby Greene jumped ship with some sea biscuits, tobacco, and a roll of cloth to barter with the native Typee tribe. Most scholars believe that Melville lived with the

Typees, rumored to be cannibals, for about a month. During this time, Melville suffered some type of leg injury, and when the wound refused to heal, Toby left to find help. Melville did not see Toby again or learn what happened to him until years later. It is his experiences among the Typee tribe that are immortalized in Melville's first novel, *Typee*. In scenes reminiscent of Paul Gauguin's paintings, Melville lived a day-to-day peaceful existence among the Typees. He soon grew tired of this unchallenging environment, however, and allowed himself to be "rescued" and brought aboard the *Lucy Ann*, an Australian whaler.

The captain of the *Lucy Ann* was ill, and the crew did no whaling. When they landed in Papeete, Tahiti, to get medical treatment, the captain transferred authority to his first mate, James German. Most of the crew hated German, and many, including Melville, refused to serve under him. In Tahiti, Melville and several shipmates mounted a failed mutiny and were imprisoned under the stewardship of "Captain Bob," a native who ran the local jail. After the *Lucy Ann* left port, without her rebels, Captain Bob allowed his prisoners to roam the islands at will. Melville met an eccentric doctor (on whom most scholars believe Dr. Long Ghost in *Omoo* is based) and the two decided to live among the natives as beachcombers. It was during these ventures that Melville became thoroughly disgusted by the Christian missionaries who attempted to convert the natives. "No race upon earth is less opposed by nature to the munitions of Christianity than the people of the South Seas. . . . They can hardly even be said to reflect," Melville wrote during this period. After traveling among the tribes of Tahiti, Melville decided to join another whaler, the *Charles & Henry*, on November 4, 1842, arranging to be discharged on the Hawaiian island of Maui. Moving on to Honolulu, Melville worked as a pin boy in a bowling alley, then as a bookkeeper, but left suddenly to avoid being arrested for desertion when the *Acushnet* pulled into port.

Melville enlisted in the U.S. Navy for a homeward voyage aboard the USS *United States*. Once again home in Boston on October 3, 1844, Melville regaled his family with his adventures, which they encouraged him to try to write down and sell.

The result was *Typee*, published in 1846. *Typee* was extremely popular; in it Melville played up the more exciting aspects of his travels, including having his main character wonder whether the Typees were cannibals. A reader from a publishing house that did not publish *Typee* wrote, "This work if not as good as *Robinson Crusoe* seems to be not far behind it."

Melville quickly followed up on the success of *Typee* by writing *Omoo*, published in 1847. And he coupled his writing career with successes in love, as well. He married Elizabeth Shaw the same year, moving to New York, where he and his new wife lived with Melville's younger brother and his wife. In New York, Melville met and befriended Evert Duyckinck, an editor for several book publishers who ran his own writing circle. Duyckinck invited Melville to borrow from his extensive library, and this is where Melville undertook his extensive literary education. He read Shakespeare, Dante, Montaigne, Coleridge, Browne, and Rabelais.

Perhaps influenced by his newly acquired intellectual friends and pursuits, Melville's next book was quite a departure from his adventure novels. *Mardi* explores the themes of passion and innocence through its hero's attraction to a dark temptress while he pursues a light-haired heroine. *Mardi* also experiments with what would later become a Melville trademark, expressing religious, philosophical, and political attitudes. Unfortunately, *Mardi*, published in 1849, failed to sell.

A GROWING FAMILY

Melville's first child, Malcolm, was born in February 1849. Perhaps the need to support a child drove Melville to abandon the flight into philosophical allegory he began in *Mardi* and return to the more adventurous style found in the first two novels. Melville wrote a straightforward novel loosely based on his trip to Liverpool in 1839. Called *Redburn*, it focuses on a young sailor's introduction to a heartless and indifferent world. In quick succession, Melville wrote *White Jacket*, which capitalized on his experiences aboard the *United States*. Although his publishers were grateful that Melville had returned to a more realistic narrative, Melville believed himself compromised by *White Jacket*'s publication. He wrote to his father-in-law that "no reputation that is gratifying to me, can possibly be achieved by either of these books. They are two *jobs*, which I have done for money— being forced to it, as other men are to sawing wood. . . . So far as I am individually concerned, and independent of my pocket, it is my earnest desire to write those sort of books which are said to 'fail.'"

Melville traveled to England to negotiate a contract for *White Jacket* with an English publisher in 1849. There he may also have gathered material on Revolutionary War figure Israel R. Potter. When Melville returned to the United States in February 1850, he brought his family to Pittsfield, Massachusetts, the family's country retreat, for a vacation and began working on the novel that would become *Moby Dick.*

MEETING HAWTHORNE

During this time Melville met fellow writer Nathaniel Hawthorne, and the two became friends. Hawthorne describes Melville as a "tolerably well-educated bear; although, in his gentler moods, there was a tenderness in his voice, eyes, mouth, in his gesture, and every indescribable manifestation, which few men could resist, and no women." Although he had probably not read much of Hawthorne's work when they met, Melville quickly read *Mosses from an Old Manse,* which he would review for Duyckinck's *Literary Messenger* as "Hawthorne and His Mosses." Melville believed he had found a soul mate in Hawthorne, seeing Hawthorne's attraction to dark themes as a reflection of his own interests. In his review, Melville writes, "Now it is that blackness in Hawthorne . . . that so fixes and fascinates me. . . . This blackness it is that furnishes the infinite obscure of his background— that background, against which Shakespeare plays his grandest conceits, the things that have made for Shakespeare his loftiest but most circumscribed renown, as the profoundest of thinkers."

Melville and Hawthorne's friendship was like a lifeline to Melville. He had been feeling increasingly isolated and unappreciated in the country, and Hawthorne seemed to not only support his work but *understand* it. Hawthorne, however, fifteen years older, seems a bit more reserved toward Melville, although scholars have a difficult time reconstructing the friendship, as Melville did not save Hawthorne's correspondence. Hawthorne's wife left a vivid description of Melville in a letter:

> I am not quite sure that I do not think him a very great man.
> . . . A man with a true, warm heart, and a soul and an intellect—with life to his finger-tips; earnest, sincere and reverent; very tender and modest. He has very keen perceptive power; but what astonishes me is, that his eyes are not large

and deep. He seems to me to see everything accurately; and how he can do so with his small eyes, I cannot tell. They are not keen eyes either, but quite undistinguished in any way. His nose is straight and rather handsome, his mouth expressive of sensibility and emotion. He is tall and erect, with an air free, brave and manly. When conversing, he is full of gesture and force, and loses himself in his subject. There is no grace or polish. Once in a while his animation gives place to a singularly quiet expression, out of these eyes to which I have objected; an indrawn, dim look, but which at the same time makes you feel that he is at that moment taking deepest note of what is before him. . . . It does not seem to penetrate through you, but to take you into itself.

Melville bought a 160-acre farm called Broadhall in Pittsfield from his Aunt Mary. With a loan from his father-in-law he moved his family, his mother, and his sisters to the new home in September 1850. Melville began to work hard on the farm, spending his time cultivating plants and repairing farm buildings, while setting up a routine of writing in the winter months. As he wrote to Hawthorne in 1851: "I have been busy . . . building and patching and tinkering away in all directions. Besides, I had my crops to get in. . . . I work myself; and at night my bodily sensations are akin to those I have so often felt before, when a hired man, doing my day's work from sun to sun."

During the winter of 1850–1851, Melville continued a friendship and correspondence with Hawthorne, who lived in nearby Salem. After rereading *The House of the Seven Gables*, Melville wrote to Hawthorne that he had admired his ability to portray "the visible truth . . . the apprehension of the absolute condition of present things as they strike the eye of the man who fears them not, though they do their worst to him."

BETWEEN THE WHALE'S FLUKES

For a year Melville labored away at his most famous novel, *Moby Dick*, which he dedicated to Hawthorne. Published in 1851, the year his second son, Stanwix, was born, the book was generally praised but condemned as blasphemous. While newspaperman Horace Greeley reviewed the book with the utmost praise, "We think it the best production which has yet come from that seething brain," another contemporary review by George Washington Peck claimed, "The rarely-imagined character has been grievously spoiled, nay altogether ruined, by a vile overdaubing with a coat of book-learning and mysticism; there is no method in his madness; and we must needs pronounce the chief feature of the volume a perfect failure, and the work itself inartistic." Apparently, Hawthorne praised the work, although his letter to Melville no longer exists. In his reply to Hawthorne's praise, Melville wrote, "Your appreciation is my glorious gratuity. . . . A sense of unspeakable security is in me at this moment, on account of your having understood the book. I have written a wicked book, and feel spotless as the lamb."

DAMN DOLLARS

The following year, 1852, Melville seems to have plunged into a state of deep moodiness, if not depression, over the failure of *Moby Dick* to provide any sort of economic security for his family. "Dollars damn me," Melville wrote to Hawthorne. He began work on *Pierre, or the Ambiguities*, reassuring his wife that he was writing a "rural bowl of milk." Unfortunately, hints of incest and a disintegrating family provoked outrage among reviewers when the book was published in 1852. *Pierre* permanently destroyed Melville's reputation in the United States, and because Melville did not allow the novel to be published in England where it may have achieved more success, the book succumbed to poor sales. Melville grew increasingly despondent and withdrawn, prompting his wife to have him examined for insanity. She tried to find Melville a steady job to ease the financial burden writing had imposed on the family, to no avail. During this period, Melville's third child, Elizabeth, was born, bringing the Melville family yet another member to support.

Melville began to contribute magazine stories to *Putnam's Monthly Magazine* and *Harper's Magazine* to make ends meet after *Moby Dick* and *Pierre* failed to generate income. The short pieces *Bartleby the Scrivener*, *The Encantadas*, and *Benito Cereno* were first published in this way. *Israel Potter* was also published serially in *Putnam's*. During the winter of 1855–1856, Melville wrote *The Confidence-Man*, perhaps his most modern and bleakest novel. His fourth child, Frances, was born in 1855. At this point, Melville suffered from deep depression and financial desperation. Forced to sell half the farm, his father-in-law saved the family from debt. When his wife despaired of living with him in this state, Melville's father-in-law proposed a four-month trip to Europe and the Middle East, hoping travel might revive Melville's spirit. On October 11, 1857, Melville sailed for Scotland. He went first to Glasgow, then to Liverpool to visit Hawthorne, then serving as U.S. consul. Hawthorne describes Melville's mood:

> We took a pretty long walk together, and sat down in a hollow among the sand hills (sheltering ourselves from the high, cool wind) and smoked a cigar. Melville, as he always does, began to reason of Providence and futurity, and of everything that lies beyond human ken, and informed me that he had "pretty much made up his mind to be annihilated" but still he does not seem to rest in that anticipation; and, I think, will never rest until he gets hold of a definite belief. It is strange how he persists—and has persisted ever since I knew him, and probably long before—in wandering to and fro over these deserts, as dismal and monotonous as the sand hills amid which we were sitting. He can neither believe, nor be comfortable in his unbelief; and he is too honest and courageous not to try to do one or the other. If he were a religious man, he would be one of the most truly religious and reverential; he has a very high and noble nature, and better worth immortality than most of us.

AN ECCENTRIC BEACHCOMBER

Melville traveled on to Egypt and Constantinople; many of his journal entries betray a resigned disappointment toward the marvels of the Holy Land. The journal includes descriptions of ruined mosques and blind men with flies crawling on their eyes, "nature feeding on men." He was grimly fascinated by Jerusalem, writing that "the diabolical landscape of Judea must have suggested to the Jewish prophets their ghastly theology. . . . Is the desolation of the land the result of the fatal embrace of the Deity?" Melville would later put these morbid reminiscences to work in his profound and lengthy poem *Clarel*, but the trip to the Middle East did nothing to lift his spirits. He then toured Europe, returned to England, and went home.

Again driven by the need to make money, Melville tried the lecture circuit between 1858 and 1860. He prepared two lectures, "Statues in Rome" and "The South Seas." Some reviewers were enthusiastic, but on the whole Melville failed to support himself with the lectures, which some reviewers claimed to be overly metaphysical and philosophical. In response to continued calls for his return to writing romances, Melville became especially cynical toward his first books, sarcastically calling them "Peedee, Hullabaloo, and Pog-

Dog." He despaired of being remembered for more than these books, once writing to Hawthorne:

> Think of it! To go down to posterity is bad enough, any way; but to go down as a "man who has lived among the cannibals"! When I speak of posterity, in reference to myself, I only mean the babies who will probably be born in the moment immediately ensuing upon my giving up the ghost. I shall go down to some of them, in all likelihood. *Typee* will be given to them, perhaps, with their gingerbread.

In 1859, a fan of the earlier books, college student Titus Coan, found him in this mood, and wrote to his mother that

> he would not repeat the experiences of which I had been reading with rapture in his books. In vain I sought to hear of Typee and those Paradise islands, but he preferred to pour forth his philosophy and his theories of life. The shade of Aristotle arose like a cold mist between myself and Fayaway. . . . With his liberal views he is apparently considered by the good people of Pittsfield as little better than a cannibal or a "beach comber."

In 1860 Melville decided to sail around the world, but the outbreak of the Civil War brought him home again. Still attempting to locate a permanent job, Melville traveled to Washington in 1861, only to return when his father-in-law died. In 1863 Melville sold the farm in Pittsfield and moved his family back to New York City. After the fall of Richmond in 1865, Melville wrote a series of poems entitled *Battle-Pieces and Aspects of the War*, published by Harpers in 1866. Sales of this work, too, proved disappointing, although today his war poetry is rated second only to Whitman's *Drum-Taps*.

Finally, in 1866, Melville found permanent work as deputy inspector in the New York Custom House. The job did not eliminate his moodiness and depression, however, and Lizzie, his wife, was so miserable that even her minister suggested she leave her husband. In the midst of this family struggle, Melville's son Malcolm killed himself by gunshot, evidently committing suicide, although publicly it was called an accident. Second son Stanwix had gone to sea and begun a lifetime of wandering that ended with his death, alone in San Francisco, in 1886.

While at the customhouse job, Melville continued to write poetry, completing his eighteen-thousand-line poem *Clarel*, which depicts a group of international travelers in the Holy Land. He filled the poem with the religious dilemmas he himself faced, including an almost hopeless attempt to believe in God in a secular world. Melville self-published *Clarel* in book form in June 1876. A failure initially, the book remains obscure to today's readers.

In 1885, with a moderate inheritance from Elizabeth's family, Melville retired from the customhouse to write, primarily poetry; his collections include *John Marr and Other Sailors*, self-published in 1888, and *Timoleon*, in 1891. His final collection, *Weeds and Wildings*, was published posthumously.

A QUIET CONTENTMENT

Melville spent the last few years of his life in obscurity, although toward the end he seems to have achieved a quiet contentment he was unable to find throughout much of his life. Highly regarded in Britain, Melville's last years were punctuated by letters from several admirers that anticipated in a very minor way that his work would one day be appreciated by millions. In 1889 Melville received one such letter from Archibald MacMeehan, Ph.D.: "For a number of years I have read and reread *Moby Dick* with increasing pleasure in every perusal: and with this study, the conviction has grown up that the unique merits of that book have never received due recognition. . . . I beg the honor of corresponding with you." Melville declined the opportunity to correspond with MacMeehan, who was planning a work of literary criticism based on *Moby Dick*, claiming that "I have lately come into possession of unobstructed leisure, but only just as, in the course of nature, my vigour sensibly declines. What little of it is left I husband for certain matters as yet incomplete, and which indeed may never be completed."

Melville was referring to his last short novel, *Billy Budd*, one of his most admired and well known works. It brings forth, with the maturity and command of Melville at the height of his writing powers, the religious and philosophical themes that obsessed him throughout his life: faith versus envy of faith, innocence versus evil, and the blindness of mankind to appreciate any of this cosmic struggle. Compelled to rework the piece again and again, Melville died in 1891 with *Billy Budd* not quite completed. The *New York Times* published this obituary: "There has died and been buried in this city, during the current week, at an advanced age, a man who is so little known, even by name, to the generation now in the vigor of life that only one newspaper contained an obituary account of him, and that of only three or four lines."

THE OTHER SIDE OF MELVILLE

A more revealing and touching commemoration of his life
was written by his granddaughter Elizabeth:

> I was not yet ten years old when my grandfather died. To put
> aside all later impressions ... results in a series of childish
> recollections, vivid homely scenes wherein he formed a pal-
> pable background for my own interested activities.
>
> Setting forth on a bright spring afternoon for a trip to Central
> Park, the Mecca of most of our pilgrimages, he made a brave
> and striking figure as he walked erect, head thrown back,
> cane in hand, inconspicuously dressed in a dark blue suit
> and a soft black felt hat. For myself, I skipped gaily beside
> him, anticipating the long jogging ride in the horse cars, the
> goats and shanty-topped granite of the upper reaches of our
> journey, the broad walks of the park, where the joy of all ex-
> istence was best expressed by running down the hills, head
> back, skirts flying in the wind. He would follow more slowly
> and call "Look out, or the 'cop' may catch you!" I always
> thought he used funny words: "cop" was surely a jollier word
> than "policeman."
>
> We never came in from a trip of this kind, nor indeed from
> any walk, but we stopped in the front hall under a coloured
> engraving of the Bay of Naples, its still blue dotted with tiny
> white sails. He would point to them with his cane and say,
> "See the little boats sailing hither and thither." "Hither and
> thither"—more funny words, thought I, at the same time a lit-
> tle awed by something far away in the tone of his voice. . . .
>
> His own room was a place of mystery and awe to me; there I
> never ventured unless invited by him. The great mahogany
> desk, heavily bearing up four shelves of dull gilt and leather
> books; the high dim book-case, topped by strange plaster
> heads that peered along the ceiling level, or bent down,
> searching blindly with sightless balls; the small black iron
> bed, covered with dark cretonne; the narrow iron grate. . . .
>
> Sad it is that he felt his grandchildren would turn against him
> as they grew older. He used to forebode as much. As it is, I have
> nothing but a remembrance of glorious fun, mixed with a
> childish awe, as of some one who knew far and strange things.

Only decades later would the world appreciate Melville's
knowledge of "far and strange things." Today, he is remembered, read, and pondered by scholars and studied and re-
discovered on a daily basis. Indeed, it seems distinctly
"Melvillian" that Herman Melville could only achieve the
fame and recognition he craved in life after his death.

CHAPTER 1

Herman Melville: An Introduction to His Works

READINGS ON

HERMAN MELVILLE

Melville as a Great Tragedian

Lewis Mumford

Lewis Mumford was an American social philosopher and educator who criticized society, especially modern technology and urban planning. His many works include a critical study entitled *Herman Melville*, from which the following article is excerpted. In it, he argues that like Shakespeare, Dostoyevsky, Dante, and other great writers, Melville chose among his themes humanity's tragic struggle against life's circumstances and elevated that struggle through his work.

Why does Herman Melville mean so much more to us than he did to his own contemporaries? What has his thought done for us, and what has his vision given?

The change that has come about is not merely a change of style.... The things that concerned Melville are, like the cubist quilts and coverlets of the 1850's, distinctly modern. ... Moby-Dick, the more closely we consider it, mounts to that lonely wind-swept plateau in whose rarefied air only the finest imaginations can breathe. Distinctly, Moby-Dick belongs with The Divine Comedy and Hamlet and The Brothers Karamazov and War and Peace; and if it does not establish its right to this company, it must occupy a lower place than the successful novels of its period, a David Copperfield or a Pendennis, books written with a complete acceptance of the current limitations and provincialities.

Melville's work, taken as a whole, expresses that tragic sense of life which has always attended the highest triumphs of the race, at the moments of completest mastery and fulfilment. Where that sense is lacking, life shrivels into small prudences and weak pleasures and petty gains, and those great feats of thought and imagination which transform the

From *Herman Melville* by Lewis Mumford. Copyright ©1929, renewed 1957 by Lewis Mumford (New York: Harcourt, Brace, 1929). Reprinted by permission of Gina Maccoby Literary Agency.

very character of the universe and relieve human purpose from the scant sufficiency of toiling and eating and sleeping, in a meaningless, reiterative round, shrivel away, too. John Ruskin saw the truth of this when, in spite of his pacifist convictions, he praised the art of war, for its effect upon the human spirit: life is intensified and purposive when the battle with the inimical forces that surround us, like Ahab's battle, is a deliberate pursuit and challenge, and not merely an apathetic waiting for a purely physiological end.

The tragedy of life, its evanescence, its frustrations, its limitations within physical boundaries almost as narrow as a straitjacket, its final extinction, becomes, in a day that consciously embraces its fate, the condition of an heroic effort. Death, which biologically is merely the terminus of a natural process, acquires significance for man because he anticipates it and modifies his activities so as to circumvent it: by memory and foresight, by choosing his ends, dreaming of immortality, erecting monuments and statues and museums, and above all, by transmitting the written word, man creates a destiny beyond his life's physical span. It is just because the worms lie in wait that man defies the gods, cherishes the images he has created and the relations he has solidified in custom and thought, and centres his efforts on those things which are least given to meaningless change. Though the sensible world is not derived, as Plato thought, from the heaven of ideas, the opposite of this is what every culture must strive for: to derive from the sensible world that which may be translated to a more durable world of forms.

THE TRAGIC STRUGGLE

Within the world of these forms there is Life, a thing of value, and not merely living, a matter of fact and habit and animal necessity. Whether one develops this tragic sense of values on a battlefield, like Sophocles, or in a whaleboat, like Melville, it is a precious experience: for living, merely living, as every profane writer from Petronius Arbiter to Theodore Dreiser has shown, brings boredom, satiety, despair: whereas Life is eternal, and he who has faith in it and participates in it is saved from the emptiness of the universe and the pointlessness of his own presence therein. Living, for man, in all but the most brutish communities, like those of the savages of the Straits of Magellan or the outcasts of a Liverpool or New York slum, includes and implies this Life;

and when Melville summons into his whaler the several races of the world, he is expressing the universal nature of that effort which caps nature with culture, existence with meaning, and facts with forms. Ahab's tragic struggle is the condition of every high endeavour of the mind, even though Death be its tragic reward; while adjustment, acquiescence, accepting outward conditions as inward necessities, though they may prolong living in the physical sense, effectually curtail Life: this attitude, the attitude of Melville's contemporaries, the attitude of the routineers and Philistines of all times—and they have never perhaps been so numerous as today—disrupts life more completely than illness and death do; for it brings about a deliquescence of forms, such as the nineteenth century showed in all its common arts, and a disintegration of human purposes. When that happens, the White Whale of brute energy reigns supreme: Life itself is denied: living produces no values, and men hide their emptiness by embracing dull counterfeits of purpose.

Melville's younger contemporaries, who fought in the Civil War, knew Life and Death; but those who prospered in the years that followed knew something more dreadful than simple death: they knew chaos and purposelessness and disintegration, such chaos and purposelessness, mixed with a wan, reminiscent hope, as Henry Adams pictured in his Education. Herman Melville portrayed a human purpose, concentrated to almost maniacal intensity, in Moby-Dick; and in Pierre and The Confidence Man, he showed the black aftermath, when the purpose was not sustained and carried out in art, and when he himself was deserted in his extremity, by contemporaries who neither understood nor heeded nor shared his vision. No single mind can hold its own against all that is foreign to it in the universe: Shakespeare's solitary heroes issue their brief defiance only to be blotted out: such unity of spirit as one may possess, as philosopher or poet, must be sustained in the community itself. Now, a new culture, the product of two hundred and fifty years of settled life in America, had produced Walden, Leaves of Grass, Emerson's Notebooks, and Moby-Dick; but that culture, instead of supporting and carrying forward the integration of man and nature and society shadowed forth in those books, was completely uprooted by the Civil War, and a material civilization, inimical in many aspects to the forms and symbols of a humane culture, was swept in by the very act of destruction.

Two generations of that material civilization have shown us its lopsidedness, its aimlessness, its grand attempt to conceal its emptiness by extending concrete roads and asphalted streets and vacuum cleaners to more and more remote terrains. Our most humane writers, like Mr. Sherwood Anderson, have proved how mercilessly the whole human being is crippled by this one-sided triumph; and even our most bewildered writers, who have exulted in all these maimed energies, have shown in their very act of deification how brutal and aimless they are. We realize that the effort of culture, the effort to make Life significant and durable, to conquer in ourselves that formidable confusion which threatens from without to overwhelm us—this effort must begin again. And in thus making a beginning we are nearer to Whitman with his cosmic faith and Melville in his cosmic defiance than we are to a good part of the work of our own contemporaries. It is not that we go back to these writers: it is, rather, that we have come abreast of them; for in creating that new synthesis, in lieu of the formless empiricisms and the rootless trancendentalisms of the last three centuries, the writers of our own classic past were nearer to the contemporary problem than almost any of the Europeans have been—since the physical remains of another culture in Europe give the mind a false sense of stability and security.

Herman Melville's world is our world, magnificently bodied and dimensioned: our synthesis must include and sublimate that very quest of power which Melville portrayed with such unique skill, as a combination of science and adventure and spiritual hardihood, in Typee, Mardi, and Moby-Dick. Melville's life warns us not to stop here: men must test their strength in surrender as well as in lonely conquest: he who knows neither social union nor sexual passion nor love is indeed an Ishmael, who finds himself an outcast because he has cast out that which was most precious to his own nature: there is love in the universe as well as power: the sun warms and the rain slakes the thirst: the whales dally and the first song of creation is the song of sex.

A SEARCH FOR SOLUTIONS TO LIFE'S PROBLEMS

The synthesis that Melville foreshadowed in his ideas is not simply a logical structure: Melville's synthesis was embodied in acts and deeds. During the years of his early manhood, as he wandered about the world and contemplated existence under the stars and bore a hand in working the ship, his environment, his experience, and his vital relationships were an integer. He did not lack what libraries and cities and the social heritage of man gives: indeed, he enjoyed fully the resources of a sound literary and philosophic scholarship; but he mixed this with activities that gave back to books the subtle properties that cannot be transmitted to the printed page, but must be derived directly from living. The reviewers in London might well have been shocked by the spectacle of a common sailor writing Typee or White-Jacket. Melville had bridged in his life that great gap between the respectable, learned professions and the common trades that had hitherto been crossed, with rare exceptions, only by those who definitely had lost caste, or who, like Burns, had risen with a sense of uneasy, sullen pride to acceptance among people of high rank.

Melville was an American—and that implied the dissolution of spiritual frontiers. America had taken all the established castes and classifications of Europe and left them to sort themselves out according to nature and ability: this was the true and beneficial result of eighteenth-century thinking and its political accompaniments. By a singular dissociation of ideas, which involved the destruction of an old social tissue, it had permitted a free and disinterested creature, a man, to emerge from a conglomeration of classes and practical interests. Melville was not primarily a sailor; he was not an adventurer; he was a man sailing, a man adventuring, a man thinking, proving in his early manhood that a whole and healthy life may involve many functions, without sacrificing its wholeness and health to any one of them. Whitman with his carpentering and his nursing, Thoreau with his pencil-making and gardening, were Herman Melville's brothers in the way and the life. They did not disdain practical life: they faced it manfully: but instead of neglecting every other activity for "business" they saw that what was called business was only a small part of the totality of living: they behaved toward it *as if it were real,* as Whitman said, with the knowledge that merely getting a living was not a sufficient contribution to Life. Brutal though Melville found whaling to be, it communicated, nevertheless, a sense of Life: there was astronomy and natural history and art and religion within the bulky hold of a whaler, as well as technics and business and the daily logbook.

The vision that grew out of this experience was a whole one, not, like the science of its time, subordinated to practical interests or even narrower metaphysical schemata. Through its dissociation from inherited values all things began at scratch: no one element in life, except sex, carried a handicap. Melville's settling down was inevitable, inevitable and difficult: but the difficulty was not due to the inability of a restless adventurer to accept a tamer and more even existence: it was due to the fact that, having known a rounded and cultured life, however savage and exacting, he could not submit to the desiccated routine of Western civilization, with its contempt for art, its gross disregard for the higher manifestations of science, its dislike for meditation, its subservient religion, its frank subordination of all other values to that of Comfort. Melville's contemporaries, with chance exceptions, neither lived as full a life as he had lived in the South Seas, nor were able to understand it, even as a theory. For these contemporaries, Melville's vision was an example of Bedlam literature: they did not realize that Bedlam was precisely the world they lived in, and that Melville's vision, like Emerson's, like Whitman's, like Thoreau's, was a part, and a great part, of a new cultural synthesis.

The stripping down of Herman Melville's ego, which he began in Mardi and finished in Pierre, was a sloughing away of labels, nicknames, party war-cries, habits, conventions, and acceptances; it was, necessarily, a prelude to that building up of a new ego, a surer and more central, a social and participating self, which is the task of our own time for both men and communities. Melville was crippled in the work of reconstruction by a hiatus in his own career, which was followed and made final by the social hiatus of the Civil War: though he sought to carry the work further in Clarel, one cannot pretend that he did anything but give a hint of this mended psyche, this more richly integrated self: one of his last poems, The Lake of Pontoosuce, perhaps approaches nearer to the goal than any other work of his. Had he built up that ego, his vision might have fully complemented Whitman's—land and sea, day and night, sunlight and shadow, triumph and tragedy. That union was latent: it is for us to effect it. It is useless, however, to speculate upon what might have been. The accidents that befell Melville, as he rounded his own Cape Horn, were part of that malign doom he himself pictured in Moby-Dick, and they do not affect the essence of his work. Whatever Melville's life was, his art in Moby-Dick exhibits that integration and synthesis which we seek. Through his art, he escaped the barren destiny of his living: he embraced Life; and we who now follow where his lonely courage led him embrace it, too. This embrace was a fertile one; and in each generation it will bring forth its own progeny. The day of Herman Melville's vision is now in the beginning. It hangs like a cloud over the horizon at dawn; and as the sun rises, it will become more radiant, and more a part of the living day.

Melville's Obsessive Hatred of God Limited His Greatness

Lawrance Thompson

In the following article, Lawrance Thompson argues that Melville's "quarrel with God" limited him as a writer. Melville, he writes, was obsessed with one theme: God is to blame for creating an unjust world. Thompson argues that this one-dimensional obsession made his works hopelessly flawed. Thompson was a professor at Princeton University and the author of works on Robert Frost, William Faulkner, and Henry W. Longfellow, and a controversial book on Melville entitled *Melville's Quarrel with God*, from which this viewpoint is excerpted.

In my analysis and interpretation of Herman Melville's art and thought, I have consciously and arbitrarily restricted my approach: I have tried to present and resolve what I see as the basic or fundamental problems posed by Melville's artistic and non-artistic attitudes toward his materials, and toward his readers; also, the related problems as to the readers' aesthetic responsibility to Melville's art. . . .

Because Melville's responses to life were what they were, he needed a scapegoat: someone to blame. Having started with hating Christians because they were not sufficiently Christian, he proceeded to hate Christians because they were Christians. When that scapegoat failed to satisfy him, he went on to hate the Calvinistic concept of God, and then proceeded to hate God. It never seemed to occur to him that he had merely declared his independence from the ideal of Calvinism in order to pledge his allegiance to an inverted form of that same ideal.

Let me say again that I am not urging that Melville should not have been inconsistent, or that he would have been a better artist if he had been more consistent. He might never have been an artist, in any sense, if he had gotten his own inner conflicts straightened out. For our aesthetic satisfaction, then, it is fortunate that Melville was exactly what he was. Nevertheless, if our ultimate concern is to understand Melville's art, there is value in recognizing how it happened that his non-artistic spiritual idiom made his artistic idiom the complex thing it certainly is.

As I see it, the major problem which confronts the reader, as he comes to Melville for the first time, is the problem of recognizing, and learning to cope with, those different forms of artistic deception and hoodwinking which he developed and employed, because of his embarrassment over the heretical and blasphemous nature of his views. . . . His own disillusionment forced him into such a private preoccupation with, and employment of, ambiguities and equivocations that he did not need to contrive any principles or practices of artistic subterfuge. It is apparent, however, that the persistent and concealed sadness of his long experience as a human being was alleviated for him by the happiness of his long experience as a literary artist: the retaliatory triumph which he achieved came to him through the act of pushing words around, to make those words do what he wanted them to do. And a very high degree of that pleasure, certainly, was derived from his skill in pushing words around in such a way that some of his readers would not understand what he wanted those words to do and say. Like his early literary idol, John Milton, he was haughty enough to be content with fit audience, though few.

LITERARY DECEPTION

Part of that major problem which confronts the first-reader of Melville is the problem of recognizing, and learning to cope with, his adaptation of moral allegory to his own peculiar uses, in such a way as to create ambiguous allegorical meanings. Once again, this adaptation of moral allegory should be recognized as a significant element in his principle and practice of literary deception. Melville knew that the allegorical mode of storytelling had so largely gone out of fashion, in his day, that many of his readers would be completely oblivious to his use of allegory in any form. That disposed of "the superficial skimmer of pages." He also knew that those readers well versed in the principles of moral allegory would naturally be the devout and unconsciously bias-bound Christian readers, who would quickly recognize his use of allegory and would instinctively prefer to make a conventional interpretation of his allegorical meanings. That disposed of a second category of readers. He also knew that his sustained irony, created by endowing allegory with sinister or inverted meanings, belonged in a "high hushed" literary tradition.... Considering this threefold appeal, I think it justifiable to call Melville's literary formula a kind of artistic triple talk. Artistically, he fulfilled his responsibilities to us, on this score; but we as readers have generally failed to pay enough attention, and in this sense we have not fulfilled our responsibilities to him. Yet, because he encouraged most of his readers to misunderstand him, perhaps things have worked out for Herman Melville, very much as he desired.

AN ODD BOOK

Melville was not appreciated by his contemporaries, who concurred that he went downhill after he wrote the adventure novels Typee *and* Omoo. *In an excerpt from a review published in London's* Literary Gazette *on December 6, 1851, a frustrated critic grapples with understanding the later novel* Moby Dick.

This is an odd book, professing to be a novel; wantonly eccentric; outrageously bombastic; in places charmingly and vividly descriptive. The author has read up laboriously to make a show of cetalogical learning. He has turned over the articles Whale, Porpoise, Cachalot, Spermaceti, Baleen, and their relatives, in every Encyclopædia within his reach.... Herman Melville is wise in this sort of wisdom. He uses it as stuffing to fill out his skeleton story. Bad stuffing it makes, serving only to try the patience of his readers, and to tempt them to wish both him and his whales at the bottom of an unfathomable sea.

Finally, we may quite easily summarize the essential element in the general range of Melville's vision, because that element remained so constant throughout so much of his later life. As I have been obliged to reiterate, the general range of Melville's vision is somewhat disappointing (not nearly so exciting and fascinating as the infinite variety of his devices for representing it) because that vision narrows down to the sharp focus of a misanthropic notion that the world was put together wrong, and that God was to blame. The gist of it is that simple. He spent his life not merely in sneering at the gullibility of human beings who disagreed with him but also in sneering at God, accusing God, up-braiding God, blaming God, and (as he thought) quarreling with God. The turn which his life had taken translated him from a transcendentalist and a mystic into an inverted transcendentalist, an inverted mystic. To this extent, then, he was consistent, in spite of all his concomitant inconsistencies, to the very end of his life. Like his own Captain Ahab, he remained a defiant rebel, even in the face of death.

Emblems delighted Melville so much (particularly when he could invert them) that his grave-stone emblem should be the Melville coat of arms, on which the motto indicates the ultimate irony of his triumphant departure from the Hell of this life:

"*Denique Caelum.*" (Heaven, at last.)

The Adventure Novels Prove Melville Is a Humorist

Edward H. Rosenberry

Literary critic Edward H. Rosenberry argues that while most people dwell on Melville's sophistication and literary density, few notice that Melville was quite a humorist. In the following selection, Rosenberry focuses on the adventure novels, *Typee, Omoo, Redburn,* and *White-Jacket,* to show how Melville uses humor to poke fun at institutions, people, and ideas. Rosenberry is professor emeritus at the University of Delaware, where he served as the chairman of the English department and acting dean of the College of Arts and Sciences. Rosenberry was also president of the Melville Society in 1981. He is the author of *Melville,* numerous articles on Melville and other American authors, and *Melville and the Comic Spirit,* from which this selection is excerpted.

The story of Melville's literary comedy begins in the racy and circumstantial pages of his first four adventure stories— *Typee, Omoo, Redburn,* and *White-Jacket.* The old delusion that these books are faithful self-portraits of the artist as a young man has been dispelled, but they remain collectively the most reliable portrait of the man as a young artist that we are likely to get. Whatever their departures from literal autobiography, they have a broad common foundation in the actual experiences of their roving author. In his reactions to certain preposterously altered orders of life across the world from Lansingburgh, New York, we can see his sense of humor most instinctively reflecting the values that color the elemental chiaroscuro of fact and fancy. . . .

Melville's adventures before the mast in the 1840's were so fraught with crudity, privation, and danger that one's hair rises at the thought of the reality behind many of his casual and ludicrous descriptions. Yet, like scores of budding Western humorists around their prairie campfires, Melville learned on midnight watches before the flaring try-works [brick furnaces holding metal pots for rendering whale oil from blubber] how whalemen "narrated to each other their unholy adventures, their tales of terror told in words of mirth." After three years of practice in sharing horrors with his shipmates and matching their mountainous comic lies about them, he was marvelously equipped to shock the mere "state-room sailors" he turned to entertain in his books. With relish he recalled the great tobacco famine on the *Highlander*, which the crew combatted by renovating their "chaws" in the ship's oven, then combing dark corners for discarded plugs, and finally settling for the "cheese-like" yarn of old ship's cable, a delicacy marred only by the tar "with which the flavour of all ropes is more or less vitiated." There is no dread, only a wry exhilaration, in his description of the nauseous *Julia*, whose forecastle was "like the hollow of an old tree going to decay" and was so overrun with cockroaches and rats that "the business of eating and drinking was better done in the dark than in the light of day." "Lucky for us Melville makes it fantastic," D.H. Lawrence has remarked. "It must have been pretty sordid." Like the fantasy-makers of the West of whom Constance Rourke tells us, Melville had swung "from an impinging terror to a gross and often brutal comedy."

The variety of terrors and hardships which Melville turned to comic account in his early books extends over a considerable range. One thinks of the "midnight misgivings" of Tommo and Toby at their first cannibal campfire, of the battle with the "small swordfish" that were the Polynesian mosquitoes, of the incredible obstacles to sleep in both the Navy and the merchant marine, of the perils of shaving, either with a dull blade in a rocking storm or with a shark's tooth in a cannibal hut. But the unmistakable keynote in Melville's comedy of hardship is a gastronomic one. The bias is evident in both the rope-yarn episode and the account of the *Julia*'s vermin. The cannibal scare of Tommo and Toby adds to this element the terror of death; but at bottom, and quite overtly as the scene progresses, the central point of attack is the digestive sensibility. When it becomes clear that the Typees are planning to feed rather than eat their guests, a new and even more plausible horror replaces the old:

> "I say, Tommo, you are not going to eat any of that mess there, in the dark, are you? Why, how can you tell what it is?"
>
> "By tasting it, to be sure," said I, masticating a morsel that Kory-Kory had just put in my mouth; "and excellently good it is too, very much like veal."
>
> "A baked baby, by the soul of Captain Cook!" burst forth Toby, with amazing vehemence; "veal! why there never was a calf on the island till you landed."

"Emetics and luke-warm water!" Melville remarks in our stead. "What a sensation in the abdominal regions!"

No qualms disturb the playfulness with which he damns the miserable fare he had managed to thrive on as a sailor. Evert Duyckinck, after reading about the grim larder of the *Dolly*, wrote to Hawthorne that Melville had actually preferred "the society of cannibals to the interminable casks of corned beef and impracticable bread which so afflicted his imagination in the hold of that vessel." It might easily have seemed so from the description in the fourth chapter of *Typee*, but, as another writer of sea stories observed with British understatement, "Melville romances somewhat when he approaches the galley; and you are scarcely sure that he means all he says." The mess of the *Julia*, on which the fictional Melville escaped from Nukuheva, was evidently worse than that of the ship that had brought him there, but its only literary effect is a heightened humor. The pork "looked as if preserved in iron rust"; the beef gave rise to a "story of a horse's hoof with the shoe on having been fished up out of the pickle"; the biscuits were "hard little gunflints, honey-combed through and through, as if the worms usually infesting this article on long tropical voyages, had, in boring after nutriment, come out at the antipodes without finding anything." The Liverpool packet on which young Redburn sailed may have had less appalling food, but the coffee it served is described with compensatory eloquence. Generally cold, and inexhaustible in its variety of bad flavors, it was prepared by an unhygienic Negro cook who was never seen to wash but once, "and that was at one of his own soup pots." Standard fare on all ships was a concoction called *duff*, "made of flour and water, and of about the consistence of an underdone brick."

The zenith—or nadir—of Melville's gastronomic humor, the episode that comes closest to turning "impinging terror" into "gross and brutal comedy," is the story of the practical

A TYPICAL DAY

In this excerpt from a letter to prominent New York editor and critic Evert Duyckinck, quoted in Willard Thorp's Herman Melville, *Melville writes about a typical day. Here he reveals the rather scathing humor that Rosenberry notes in his article.*

I have a sort of sea-feeling here in the country, now that the ground is all covered with snow. I look out of my window in the morning when I rise as I would out of a port-hole of a ship in the Atlantic. My room seems a ship's cabin; & at nights when I wake up & hear the wind shrieking, I almost fancy there is too much sail on the house, & I had better go on the roof & rig in the chimney.

Do you want to know how I pass my time?—I rise at eight—thereabouts—& go to my barn—say good-morning to the horse, & give him his breakfast. (It goes to my heart to give him a cold one, but it can't be helped) Then, pay a visit to my cow—cut up a pumpkin or two for her, & stand by to see her eat it—for its a pleasant sight to see a cow move her jaws—she does it so mildly & with such a sanctity.—My own breakfast over, I go to my work-room & light my fire—then spread my M.S.S. on the table—take one business squint at it, & fall to with a will. At 2½ P.M. I hear a preconcerted knock at my door, which (by request) continues till I rise & go to the door, which serves to wean me effectively from my writing, however interested I may be. My friends the horse & cow now demand their dinner—& I go & give it them. My own dinner over, I rig my sleigh & with my mother or sisters start off for the village—& if it be a Literary World day, great is the satisfaction thereof.—My evenings I spend in a sort of mesmeric state in my room—not being able to read—only now & then skimming over some large-printed book.—Can you send me about fifty fast-writing youths, with an easy style & not averse to polishing their labors? If you can, I wish you would, because since I have been here I have planned about that number of future works & cant find enough time to think about them separately.

But I dont know but a book in a man's brain is better off than a book bound in calf—at any rate it is safer from criticism. And taking a book off the brain, is akin to the ticklish & dangerous business of taking an old painting off a panel —you have to scrape off the whole brain in order to get at it with due safety—& even then, the painting may not be worth the trouble.

joke played on Surgeon Cuticle by the wardroom officers in *White-Jacket.*

> Once [it begins] when they had some sago pudding for dinner, and Cuticle chanced to be ashore, they made up a neat parcel of this bluish-white, firm, jelly-like preparation, and placing it in a tin box, carefully sealed with wax, they deposited it on the gun-room table, with a note, purporting to come from an eminent physician in Rio, ... begging leave to present the scientific Senhor Cuticle—with the donor's compliments—an uncommonly fine specimen of a cancer.

SELF-RIDICULE

... Self-ridicule, in the halcyon atmosphere of *Typee, Omoo, Redburn,* and *White-Jacket,* is for the most part purely jocular. The richest vein occurs in *Redburn,* not unnaturally, since the theme of the book is the practical education of a greenhorn. But the attitude is maintained as consistently, if with less concentration, in the other narratives. One strongly anti-romantic episode in *Omoo* is characteristic of Melville's gleeful exposures of his own punctured pride. Languishing in the stocks of a makeshift Tahitian prison, Melville and his fellow mutineers from the *Julia* are mortified by a stream of native sight-seers and particularly by one light-minded beauty, who laughs and points at each successive absurdity sprawled before her. Melville determines to stifle her ridicule with a show of manly dignity.

> Ere her glance fell upon me, I had, unconsciously, thrown myself into the most graceful attitude I could assume, leaned my head upon my hand, and summoned up as abstracted an expression as possible. Though my face was averted, I soon felt it flush, and knew that the glance was on me: deeper and deeper grew the flush, and not a sound of laughter.
>
> Delicious thought! she was moved at the sight of me. I could stand it no longer, but started up. Lo! there she was; her great hazel eyes rounding and rounding in her head, like two stars, her whole frame in a merry quiver, and an expression about the mouth that was sudden and violent death to anything like sentiment.

In some such light-hearted vein Melville treats every instance in which he appears in these books as the traditional "goat"—every instance, that is, but one. The occasion is young Redburn's departure from home on a river boat, a ragged, hungry pauper, armed with a fowling piece to be pawned for sea-togs, and a single dollar to pay his boat fare. He becomes a "goat" when he discovers that the fare has gone up to two dollars and that he is reduced to still more abject disgrace before his fashionable fellow-travelers, who have already been eyeing his patches askance.

> I stood their gazing some time, but at last could stand it no more. I pushed my seat right up before the most insolent gazer, a short fat man, with a plethora of cravat around his neck, and fixing my gaze on his, gave him more gazes than he sent. This somewhat embarrassed him, and he looked around for someone to take hold of me; but no one coming, he pretended to be very busy counting the gilded wooden beams overhead. I then turned to the next gazer, and clicking my gun-lock, deliberately presented the piece at him.
>
> Upon this, he oversat his seat in his eagerness to get beyond my range, for I had him point-blank, full in the left eye; and several persons starting to their feet, exclaimed that I must be crazy. So I was at that time; for otherwise I know not how to account for my demoniac feelings.

It is the first dramatic instance we have of the peculiar perversity of humor which Melville so suggestively labels for us as "demoniac." The episode is striking here because of its singularity in the midst of a sunnier humor, but it was destined to cast a long shadow after it.

Around the central self-portrait Melville's memory drew, with comic distortion, the myriad figures that had peopled his transposed frontier world. Fortunately, Melville's forte, like every true humorist's, was the human comedy, and it is to the enduring humor of his portraiture, more than anything else, that the survival of his "popular" novels is due. The raw material was perfect, and the artist evidently knew what it was good for. "At sea a fellow comes out," he wrote to Duyckinck years later. "Salt water is like wine, in that respect." The young Melville simply capitalized on a matchless opportunity to study all kinds of men under the influence of both salt water and wine, frequently both at once. The resulting gallery is heavy in rogues, most of them at sea and most of them drunk, but some merely at sea or merely drunk, and a few even on land and sober. . . .

Redburn, despite Melville's apparent contempt for it, is anything but "beggarly" in the caliber of its salt-fed comic portraiture. One searches very nearly in vain, before *Moby-Dick*, for anything surpassing the sure, full-bodied artistry displayed in the sketches of the cook, the steward, and Jack Blunt. The *Highlander*'s cook takes on a more memorable charm than his coffee and his grooming would suggest. Behind an imposing façade of doormat, knocker, and name-plate, the devout "Mr. Thompson" presides with sovereign dignity over his stove-filled cubicle, earnestly poring over a greasy Bible as he stirs his pots, but occasionally forgetting his piety with a high sea running in his firebox. His boon companion is the mulatto steward, an ex-Broadway barber named Lavender, who perfumes his hair, affects a glass "diamond" and a turban, reads sentimental novels, and wears cast-off clothing "in the height of exploded fashions." It is the incontestable hand of an artist that brings these two together to finish their own portraits by the mutual illumination of their humors:

> And sometimes Mr. Thompson would take down his Bible, and read a chapter for the edification of Lavender, whom he knew to be a sad profligate and gay deceiver ashore; addicted to every youthful indiscretion. He would read over to him the story of Joseph and Potiphar's wife; and hold Joseph up to him as a young man of excellent principles, whom he ought to imitate, and not be guilty of his indiscretion any more. And Lavender would look serious, and say that he knew it was all true—he was a wicked youth, he knew it—he had broken a good many hearts, and many eyes were weeping for him even then, both in New York, and Liverpool, and London, and Havre. But how could he help it? He hadn't made his handsome face, and fine head of hair, and graceful figure. It was not *he*, but the others, that were to blame; for his bewitching person turned all heads and subdued all hearts, wherever he went. And then he would look very serious and penitent, and go up to the little glass, and pass his hands through his hair, and see how his whiskers were coming on.

Jack Blunt, who comes in for a somewhat fuller treatment in the next chapter, is that rare gift to the humorist, the happy sucker. A devotee of fortune-telling, "Balm of Paradise" hair oil, miscellaneous quack pills, and mathematical horoscopes, Blunt is also God's gift to the confidence man; but the gentle whimsicality with which Melville here handles both the fleecer and the fleeced stands in striking contrast to the acerbity of the book he was one day to write on that special theme. . . .

DEDICATED DRINKERS

The majority of Melville's sailors are dedicated drinkers. Some are the heroic type who, like Mad Jack of the *Neversink*, seem to have been "suckled at a puncheon [cask]." Some are the narcotic type, maintaining, like the pilot at

Nukuheva, "that interesting state of intoxication when a man is amiable and helpless." All are men of little discretion and no shame at all; according to Redburn's prim characterization, they "only blush after the third bottle." The degree of their dedication may have been a matter of sober regret to Melville. He suggests as much in his assertion that the Navy was an "asylum for drunkards . . . driven back to the spirit-tub and the gun-deck by [their] old hereditary foe, the ever-devilish god of grog." As an artist, however, he wrung a good deal of excellent comedy from it. Writing of those very man-of-war's men he pitied for their addiction, he made a good thing of the occasion when the grog gave out on the *Neversink*. Deprived of their daily tot, the crew suffered an alarming slump in morale until ten curiously stiff and sweet-smelling fellows were laid out in the brig to sleep off a mysterious drunkenness, and it became known below decks that the ship's store was amply supplied with Eau de Cologne.

> The news spread far and wide among the men, being only kept secret from the officers and underlings, and that night the long, crane-necked Cologne bottles jingled in out-of-the-way corners and by-places, and, being emptied, were sent flying out of the ports. With brown sugar, taken from the mess-chests, and hot water begged from the galley-cooks, the men made all manner of punches, toddies, and cocktails, letting fall therein a small drop of tar, like a bit of brown toast, by way of imparting a flavour. . . . Next day, fore and aft, the whole frigate smelled like a lady's toilet.

Even Melville's own disapproval of intemperance is turned to comic account in *Redburn*, where he portrays himself as a member of the "Juvenile Total Abstinence Association," driven to apostasy by being seasick among a crew well stocked with the standard cure, "which they had brought along to sea with them, *to taper off with*, as they called it." . . .

MELVILLE POKES FUN AT SEX

Sex, the universal joke, is a recurrent theme in the writing of Melville's jocular-hedonic period. It appears most unreservedly in *Omoo*, under the combined influence of Long Ghost and the free-and-easy mores of the islands, where "the best dress in courting is motley" and the courtesies of hospitality may be extended by a native hostess "to a degree altogether superfluous." Even in the absence of these priming influences its persistence reflects the normality of

Melville's masculine bias and adds to the comic zest of his early books. In *Pierre* he was to take on a new gravity in dealing with intersexual relations, but until then his literary women were no more than a piquant diversion. Melville on his canoeing excursions in *Typee* sounds a good deal like Long Ghost on his botanical ones: "But I was ever partial to what is termed in the *Young Men's Own Book*—'the society of virtuous and intelligent young ladies;' and in the absence of the mermaids, the amusement became dull and insipid." Thus we are introduced to the famous *affaire* Fayaway, which, notwithstanding its theatrical romanticism and careful narrative propriety, is essentially a gambol on the part of a Male Animal frankly stimulated by a young lady's smoking, standing naked in a canoe, and otherwise wearing a dress which "began at the waist, and terminated sufficiently far above the ground to reveal the most bewitching ankle in the universe."

Elsewhere the rovings of the healthy masculine eye are chronicled in an even more clearly picaresque mood. When, in *Omoo*, the author caught sight of a beautiful girl on horseback, he promptly enlisted Long Ghost, identified the young lady as the wife of an English planter ("happy dog"), and undaunted by that intelligence, put in an appearance at the plantation with a view to making her acquaintance. There they were graciously entertained by the lady's husband, who appealed to their secondary weaknesses by offering them fresh melons filled with sherry. "Now this was extremely polite in Mr. Bell," says Melville, keeping his eye on the ball; "still, we came to see *Mrs.* Bell." A similar incident in *Redburn*, allowing for a more appropriate naïveté in the telling, achieves its comic effect by the same subordination of lesser appetites. Attracted to an English cottage by three beautiful girls, young Redburn rises to the challenge of a suspicious mother and talks himself into an invitation to tea, where even the presence of fresh milk and "such buttered muffins [as] never were spread on the other side of the Atlantic" fails to deflect his interest. "There they sat—the charmers, I mean—eating those buttered muffins in plain sight. I wished I was a buttered muffin myself.". . .

The common stratum of material that underlay the autobiographical romances lent itself by and large to the jocular-hedonic air to which Melville was both inclined and committed in works of popular entertainment.

Melville's Short Stories Prove His Greatness as a Writer

Q.D. Leavis

Q.D. Leavis argues that Melville's short stories "are some of the finest . . . short stories in the language." He contends that the shorter works show Melville as a great humorist, social commentator, and novel thinker. Leavis is a literary critic and author of *Fiction and the Reading Public*, as well as a contributor to the anthology *New Perspectives on Melville*, from which this viewpoint is excerpted.

Julian Hawthorne wrote in an otherwise percipient reminiscence of Melville's character and disposition that 'His later writings are incomprehensible'. This from [Nathaniel] Hawthorne's son, who had presumably been initiated into the meaning and method of his father's work and so should have had some insight at least into that art which derived from Hawthorne's, suggests how inevitable it was that Melville could find no public for his fiction after his early phase as a writer of adventure books about voyages by sea. Even the incomparable *Benito Cereno* made no real impact in America in Melville's long lifetime.

But to the modern English and American reader, well trained in practical criticism and knowing with regard to myth, symbol, allegory and imagery, the writings of the great 1853–6 phase are of more interest than the earlier novels, evidently more accomplished as art, more varied—written in the short space of three years and with desperate need of money, they show an astonishing range of subject-matter, attitude, tone and style—and are noticeably more condensed, controlled and mature than either *Moby-Dick* or *Pierre*, the two previous major works; and this in spite of the discouraging fact that even *Moby-Dick* had not been a finan-

From "Melville: The 1853–56 Phase" by Q.D. Leavis, in *New Perspectives on Melville*, edited by Faith Pullin (Kent, OH: Kent State University Press, 1978). Copyright ©1978 by Edinburgh University Press. Reprinted by permission of the Kent State University Press.

cial success while *Pierre* had been and remained a dead loss. Yet Melville rallied from the disappointment, though it seriously affected his health, and triumphantly wound up this last phase of prose creativeness with an ironic masterpiece, *The Confidence-Man.* But in order to understand this difficult and still highly controversial work one must, it seems to me, have grasped the nature of the tales written while he was gestating the novel. Published mostly in magazines, they were reprinted as *The Piazza Tales* and reveal his interests and preoccupations in these fertile years as well as the kinds of technique he was inventing for these new purposes.

THE ENCANTADAS

The Encantadas is simply a series of ten sketches which have as unifying theme the horrors of a tropical waterless Nature which sustains only equally infernal forms of animal and human existence. They show how Melville's imagination at this period was haunted by the memory of the histories of the wretched castaways with their inhuman treatment by fellow-men who exceed them in cruelty. This culminates in the history of the poor half-breed woman Hunilla, treacherously deserted with her family by the captain committed to returning for them and, as sole survivor, raped by whaleboatmen to whom she looked for rescue. A pious Catholic, Hunilla had the fortitude to preserve her sanity and faith. Melville concludes her history with Hunilla riding away Christ-like on an ass, eyeing 'the beast's armorial cross', and 'Humanity, thou strong thing, I worship thee, not in the laureled victor, but in this vanquished one'—an affirmation of faith, in humanity at least and in spite of its worst manifestations, which must not be overlooked in any discussion of Melville's attitude to God and man at this period.

The others really are integral tales. They fall into groups, for instance three double tales each consisting of a contrasted pair. . . . These all spring from experiences in England and America that aroused Melville's generous indignation at social conditions—treatment of the poor, class snobbery extending even to religious worship, and surprisingly, in view of the exclusion of women from his previous novels except as ideas in *Pierre* and *Mardi,* to the treatment of women, who are seen as victims of Nature as well as of man and society. Thus in these years Melville was manifesting a considerable degree of emotional and moral involvement in social life on land, both in England and America. In *The Piazza Tales* we are not living in 'The World in a Man-of-War' as in *White-Jacket* or in the world in a whaling-ship as in *Moby-Dick*, but are taken into the full living world of the Anglo-American mid-nineteenth century, a very great step forward for Melville as an artist into the complexities of living, even, into the difficulties of family life for the man and the artist. We remember that Melville was married in 1847 and by now had children, a family to support, and was living in a household that contained also his mother and three of his sisters, a concentration of women with claims on him that inevitably forced on his attention the woman's point of view, and which also obliged him to reconsider the man's role as individual (as in *I and My Chimney*), and as artist tormented by the rival claims of his work and the support of his family.

BARTLEBY

The tale of *Bartleby the Scrivener* (1853) has received plenty of critical attention and there is no disagreement as to its meaning and the nature of its techniques, which present no difficulty. But recognition has not been given to the fact that it is one of Melville's try-outs and not an adopted position, much less a personal admission of neurosis. This is the only tale of the batch that ends in limbo. Bartleby is posited as the man who adopts a consistently negative response to the demands of unsatisfactory living in the Wall Street society (copying while facing a blank wall). His unshakable 'I would prefer not to' which he persists in until it inevitably leaves him dead of starvation in prison, with 'peering out upon him the eyes of murderers and thieves', is yet felt, like Hunilla's tragedy, to be a triumph of the indomitable spirit: Bartleby, even the lawyer his employer feels, is at rest 'with kings and counselors'. Melville himself concludes with 'Ah, Bartleby! Ah, humanity!' which is unfathomably ambiguous, perhaps a sad recognition of the human condition. Bartleby's suicidal choice is not so much the centre of Melville's attention as the complex reaction to it of his employer, whose mixture of exasperation and pity in his efforts first to save Bartleby and failing this, to wash his hands of him—all too human—are examined not without sympathy. For what could be done for a Bartleby? Can one envisage a society composed of Bartlebies? . . . Bartleby's having been a clerk in the Dead

Letter Office, and then a mere copyist of other people's compositions, are not very obscure references to the kind of literary non-life Melville saw he himself would be relegated to in all likelihood after the failure of *Pierre* and the destruction by fire in 1853 of the plates of all his novels, and with the increasing weakness of his eyesight (like Bartleby's). Not surprisingly, several tales of this period are discussions of the problem of the artist who has to earn a living in mid-nineteenth-century America—*Cock-a-Doodle-Doo!*, *The Fiddler*, *I and My Chimney*. Only two years before (1851) Melville had praised Hawthorne for as an artist always 'saying No! in thunder'—'the Devil himself cannot make him say *yes*'—and had since been inclined to castigate all those who do say *yes*, an indication of the line Melville was to explore systematically in *The Confidence-Man*. Characteristically, Melville had proceeded from his ardent endorsement of Hawthorne's apparent attitude to testing its validity by actualizing it in the case of a consistent practitioner, Bartleby, when he recognizes that however heroic it is impracticable; Bartleby's employer, the average citizen, had always been convinced, he says, that 'the easiest way of life is the best', which though ignoble is a means of survival, we see. And a year after *Bartleby* Melville tried out such an alternative to Bartleby's in an odd short sketch *The Fiddler*.

This opens with the despair of the narrator, a poet named Helmstone: 'So my poem is damned, and immortal fame is not for me! Intolerable fate!' But he is 'instantly soothed' by being introduced to the amiable and winning genius Hautboy (presumably meaning 'a high-flier') whose fame has passed and his fortune with it. But he is quite content to drudge for a living by teaching the fiddle: '*With* genius and *without* fame, he is happier than a king', his friend Standard (the average man) assures Helmstone, who feels 'I wish I were Hautboy'. So he tears up his manuscripts and follows this model's example. The tale is merely an annotation of an idea and has none of the convincing detail, the sensitive complexity and the involved technical devices Melville found necessary for the more substantial tales, showing he did not entertain this alternative very seriously. I simply cite it as another proof that his mind worked from theory to posited embodiments in alternative forms of life (like Dickens). For these he drew equally on incidents in his own experience, on documents and historical facts, and on the lives of real people, thus doing his best to keep his theorizing in touch with actuality and to direct his abstract thinking on to the life of the individual and the welfare of society.

COCK-A-DOODLE-DOO!

Nearly a year before, Melville had published the very remarkable tale *Cock-a-Doodle-Doo!* In this case Melville took off from Wordsworth's poem *Resolution and Independence* which must have exasperated him since, starting from reflections of a kind relevant to Melville's own position, on the disastrous fate of poets who from beginning in gladness pass through despondency to madness owing to poverty, Wordsworth apparently found arguments in the fortitude of the Leech-gatherer for reassurance and trust in Providence. To Melville, in debt, and in fear of blindness and possibly also of the madness from which his father died, such optimism was superficial. Accordingly, his tone in this tale is harsh and jeering. He exhibits in refutation of Wordsworth the painful history of Merrymusk (that is, 'Merry Music', creative genius) and his family, the tale being for the most part a rude parody of the poem. The narrator, in financial trouble himself and not finding comfort in Nature like Wordsworth, is cheered by the 'prodigious exulting strains' of a cock which ring through the whole countryside and throw him into a rapturous, buoyant state. It turns out to be owned by a desperately poor but dignified wood-sawyer who proudly declares: 'I raised it'. He calls it Trumpet and it crows only at his command—evidently the voice of his art which, while it can't bring him an income, makes up to him and his sick wife and children for their deprivations in material things. The narrator watches them all die happy in hearing to the last the 'glorious and rejoicing crow' of their unique Trumpet. This part is not satiric: the uncomplaining wife is heroic in her 'long-loving sympathy' with her husband, and as for the four children—listening to the cock 'Their faces shone celestially through grime and dirt. They seemed children of emperors and kings, disguised'. Merrymusk himself insists as he dies that he and all of them are well, 'in a kind of wild ecstacy of triumph over ill'. Last of all Trumpet dies, and the narrator buries them all in one grave with on the gravestone 'a lusty cock in act of crowing' and the possibly unironic inscription 'O death, where is thy sting? O grave, where is thy victory?' and—reverting now to the original tone—ends: 'and never since then have I felt the doleful dumps'.

A SMOKED HUMAN HEAD

This excerpt is taken from a review of Typee *written by author Nathaniel Hawthorne and published in the Salem, Massachusetts,* Advertiser *on March 25, 1846. Hawthorne praises the book, pointing out the wide range of experiences Melville writes about.*

The book is lightly but vigorously written; and we are acquainted with no work that gives a freer and more effective picture of barbarian life, in that unadulterated state of which there are now so few specimens remaining. . . . On one page, we read of manners and modes of life that indicate a whole system of innocence and peace; and on the next, we catch a glimpse of a smoked human head, and the half-picked skeleton of what had been (in a culinary sense) a *well-dressed* man. The author's descriptions of the native girls are voluptuously colored, yet not more so than the exigencies of the subject appear to require. He has that freedom of view—it would be too harsh to call it laxity of principle—which renders him tolerant of codes of morals that may be little in accordance with our own; a spirit proper enough to a young and adventurous sailor.

I have never encountered an explanation of why Merrymusk should have named his cock 'Trumpet'. My own conjecture is that Melville had several poems of Wordsworth's, besides *Resolution and Independence*, in his mind when composing this tale, all of them having in common the theme of the poet's creative powers. So Wordsworth's sonnet on The Sonnet was brought in by naming Merrymusk's art after what Wordsworth tells us was the favourite poetic form of great poets, as of Wordsworth himself; and the account culminates in Milton's use of the sonnet, when

> In his hand
> The Thing became a trumpet; whence he blew
> Soul-animating strains—alas, too few!

So in this complex and subtly Wordsworthian tale, which is surprisingly like D.H. Lawrence in tone and content, Melville registers belief in the sustaining and revivifying power of art, and in support of my interpretation we note that the rustic humour and scoffing tone are abandoned whenever the narrator confronts the Merrymusk household. And he is genuinely disturbed by the mighty power of Trumpet: 'the cock frightened me, like some overpowering angel in the Apocalypse'—as well as sincerely humbled by the character of Merrymusk who denies he deserves pity, declaring with superb conviction:

> Why call *me* poor? Don't the cock *I* own glorify this otherwise inglorious, lean, lantern-jawed land? Didn't *my* cock encourage *you*? And *I* give you all this glorification away gratis. I am a great philanthropist. I am a rich man—a very rich man, and a very happy one. Crow, Trumpet.

The narrator admits he 'was not wholly at rest concerning the soundness of Merrymusk's views of things, though full of admiration for him. I was thinking on the matter before my door, when I heard the cock crow again. Enough. Merrymusk is right. Oh, noble cock! oh, noble man!'

Note that New England is envisaged here as a Puritan; that is to say, the land of Puritan settlers was ignorant of art though desperately in need of it. Also, it is unable to appreciate art—no one in the countryside but the narrator and the Merrymusk family is able to hear the cock, a sly touch. An 'inglorious land' indeed! An interpretation that, because the rest can't hear the cock, the voice is imaginary and Melville trying to come to terms with a neurosis; or alternatively, that 'cock' being a sex-term the tale must be understood as a sexual *double-entendre*—are equally instances of perverse critical sophistry. The identification of cocks with poets is made beyond doubt by Melville's parody of Wordsworth's lines (at the end of the seventh stanza of *Resolution and Independence*) on the sad history of poets:

> Of fine mornings,
> We fine lusty cocks begin our crows in gladness;
> But when eve does come we don't crow quite so much,
> For then cometh despondency and madness.

And in his description of the cock's crow we see the characteristics of his own literary voice: 'full of pluck, full of fire, full of fun, full of glee. It plainly says—"*Never say die!*"'

Merrymusk then is Melville's idea of a more convincing model for Wordsworth's Leech-gatherer and he is also, with his inspiring voice Trumpet, Melville the artist (who thought of himself as poet-novelist)—we are told Merrymusk had been first a sailor, then a small farmer, and was now a hired drudge, Melville's own history. The story of the family dying prematurely as they do from harrowing poverty is surely an ironic comment on Wordsworthian trust, carrying on the ridicule with which the tale started. There is also satire in the reiterated fact that the baseless self-confidence the cock's crowing gives the narrator inspires him to reckless financial behaviour and evidently future ruin. Yet there is no doubt that Trumpet is 'the cheerer', and when he perches on the sick children's bed 'All their wasted eyes gazed at him with a wild and spiritual delight. They seemed to sun themselves in the radiant plumage of the cock'. This is sincere and moving. Melville seems to be trying to explain that though the dolours of the poet's life of poverty that Wordsworth brushes aside are inescapable and bear hardest on his family, *yet* they all, and everyone else in the world too, have thereby the consolations of art which can make life blissful and suffering negligible. The artist's support therefore can only be looked for in his sense of achievement, Melville argues.

Wordsworth's 1815 sonnet to the unfortunate painter Haydon is another that Melville seems to me to have drawn on as a help to expressing his theme in *Cock-a-Doodle-Doo!* It is next but one to the 'Trumpet' sonnet in the 1849–50 edition of Wordsworth's poems and is of such importance in elucidating Melville's argument and the conclusion we should extract that I will cite it in full:

High is our calling, Friend!—Creative Art
(Whether the instrument of words she use,
Or pencil pregnant with ethereal hues,)
Demands the service of a mind and heart,
Though sensitive, yet, in their weakest part,
Heroically fashioned—to infuse
Faith in the whispers of the lonely Muse,
While the whole world seems adverse to desert.
And, oh! when Nature sinks, as oft she may,
Through long-lived pressure of obscure distress,
Still to be strenuous for the bright reward
And in the soul admit of no decay,
Brook no continuance of weak-mindedness—
Great is the glory, for the strife is hard!

It is important to note that in these tales Melville shows he is as much concerned as Henry James or Hawthorne with the problems of the life of the artist and the necessity of art for the life of the spirit, because we must also note that these considerations are completely absent from the picture of life in the America of the 1850s drawn for *The Confidence-Man* shortly after. Something he knew to be central and vital has there been deliberately omitted. And these tales, particularly the complex *Cock-a-Doodle-Doo!*, show the kind of difficulty we are faced with in reading these later Melville works. The complexity does not disguise the meaning but it shows that several meanings are intended which, united, provide the means of arriving at a just conclusion. He is in his creative activity exploring all the possibilities in a given human problem, facing and considering them in turn and playing one off against the other, the changes of tone and direction giving us guide-lines. Thus in these tales he developed the method he was to need for *The Confidence-Man*, and one may well feel that tales like *Bartleby*, *Benito Cereno*, *Cock-a-Doodle-Doo!* and *The Tartarus of Maids* are almost inexhaustible. . . .

In none of the tales of this period can I find any justification for Hawthorne's opinion (*English Notebooks*, 20 November 1856) that Melville's 'writings, for a long while past, have indicated a morbid state of mind'. In *I and My Chimney* (published 1855) there is reassuring good-humour in the narrator's recognition that the women of his family suspect the soundness of his home's exceptionally tall and finely-wrought chimney, resent its bulk and mysterious foundations, which they fancy must contain a secret chamber with hidden treasure, and believe that the house would be safer and more comfortable without such a chimney. They torment the old man by getting in 'a master-mason' to test it and arrange if unsound for its removal, but the narrator circumvents them all. He has explained that the chimney 'is my backbone', 'the one grand permanence of this abode' and that 'when all the house shall have crumbled from it, this chimney will still survive'. The tale ends: 'I and my chimney will never surrender'. Thus the chimney is a composite symbol standing, apparently, for his morale, his immortal soul (which he is determined to call his own), the source of his creative power (the chimney's foundations are buried in darkness, deep down), his intellect, his personality, and his inherited traditions (a kinsman named Dacres—that is, 'Sacred'—built the house); the chimney also seems to stand, like the personal tree in European folk-tales, for his life-force, for it is sinking into the ground and crumbling as he himself grows old. This is one of Melville's most intimate and most suggestive tales. It is surely also good proof of its author's mental health. There is much wry amusement at the narrator's situation and some sympathy for the wife,

misguided though she is, who has to put up with the disad-
vantages of living with an obstinately conservative and pri-
vacy-loving intellectual, one resigned to old age and death
but not to interference with his essential self.

In short, it must be generally recognized that the tales of
Melville are some of the finest *contes* and short stories in the
language, as well as some of the most original, and that, like
D.H. Lawrence and Hawthorne, his claim to stature as an
artist is to be based on his tales at least as much as on his
novels.

The Bible in Melville's Work

Nathalia Wright

In the following selection, Nathalia Wright argues
that Melville not only makes extensive use of biblical
quotations and anecdotes in his books, but also patterns many of his characters after personages in the
Bible. Wright gives several examples of Melville's use
of the Bible and concludes that Melville intended to
correlate his characters' struggles with those of biblical heroes. A professor of English, Wright has written *Horatio Greenough: The First American Sculptor,*
American Novels in Italy, and *Melville's Use of the*
Bible, from which this article is excerpted.

In all that Melville wrote he was no nearer saying what he
had to say at the end than he was at the beginning. His effect, like Shakespeare's, is one of extension rather than of
volume. One receives the impression of spaces and dis-
tances, of approaches and retreats, of vistas opened but not
entered upon. One is always traveling but never arrives. . . .

Above all, one is made to feel that what has been left un-
said is unspeakably vaster than what has been said. The su-
perabundance of material appalls him, and he is driven at
last to think of all truth as voiceless and of the question as
more final than any answer. "God keep me from ever completing anything," cries Ishmael. "This whole book is a
draught—nay, but the draught of a draught.". . .

To this desire to extend the scope of his work, to this fear
of appearing final, all Melville's rhetorical devices and all
his voluminous sources are subservient. So indiscriminately
are they introduced and associated that they tend at last to
lose their separate identities. They are but fragments of a
boundless creation, undistinguished otherwise in the hands
of its creator. Of them all, however, no single one so far ex-

From Nathalia Wright, *Melville's Use of the Bible.* Copyright 1947, Duke University
Press, Durham, N.C. Reprinted with permission.

tends the bounds of what Melville wrote as the Bible. However he alluded to it he was assured of a contrast with his immediate material: between the common and the great, the present and the past, the natural and the supernatural. And though each is a contrast achieved by many other means as well, only this one enabled him to make them all simultaneously, at once magnifying his characters and their affairs, establishing for the briefest moment a background of antiquity, and suggesting the presence of yet another, unseen world beyond the vast scene which meets the eye.

Originally and essentially, of course, all Melville's material is simple and commonplace, becoming transformed through a marvelous imagination. Viewed strictly in the light of fact his characters are of limited powers and lowly station. Yet as their lives unfold in passion and in problem, they seem to be supermen, inhabiting a world one degree larger than life. The effect is deliberate, and it is deliberately more than the general exaggeration of his pen. Thus did he justify it [in *Moby-Dick*]:

> If, then, to meanest mariners, and renegades and castaways, I shall hereafter ascribe high qualities, though dark; weave round them tragic graces; if even the most mournful, perchance the most abased, among them all, shall at times lift himself to the exalted mounts; if I shall touch that workman's arm with some ethereal light; if I shall spread a rainbow over his disastrous set of sun; then against all mortal critics bear me out in it, thou just Spirit of Equality, which hast spread one royal mantle of humanity over all my kind! Bear me out in it, thou great democratic God! who didst not refuse to the swart convict, Bunyan, the pale, poetic pearl; Thou who didst clothe with doubly hammered leaves of finest gold, the stumped and paupered arm of old Cervantes; Thou who didst pick up Andrew Jackson from the pebbles; who didst hurl him upon a war-horse; who didst thunder him higher than a throne! Thou who, in all Thy mighty, earthly marchings, ever cullest Thy selectest champions from the kingly commons; bear me out in it, O God!

This effect of magnitude in Melville's characters is achieved largely by figurative language, since his imagery contains references to so many great personages of history and literature. Side by side with the nameless crews of his ships walk Henry VIII, Charlemagne, Xerxes, Apis, Ammon, Jove, Perseus, Prometheus, Mohammed, Faust, Hamlet, Beelzebub, Abraham. With many of them Melville briefly compared his own characters: Daggoo and Hivohitee to

Ahasuerus, Jarl at his supper to Belshazzar at his feast, the helmsman of the *Highlander* to Ixion, General McPherson to Sarpedon, the carpenter at his forge to Prometheus, Ahab to Adam: "'I feel deadly faint, bowed, and humped, as though I were Adam, staggering beneath the piled centuries since Paradise.'" The Bible, in fact, provides genealogies to ennoble the meanest of men, for all, it asserts in various accounts, are descendants of the Jehovah-created Adam, of the sons of God who intermarried with the daughters of men, of the patriarch Noah, and spiritually of the New Testament Father. Melville cited them all.

More important . . . is the deeper relationship which is made to exist between some of these personages and Melville's characters, whereby the patterns of their lives are both clarified and given significance. Some of them are named for the great, and thus the parallel moves with them: a whaling captain for a king of Israel, a Revolutionary soldier for Jehovah's chosen people, a sailor for the son of a patriarch, another sailor for a Norse jarl [nobleman], two lunatics for a prophet and an archangel, a religious fanatic for the rebuilder of Jerusalem, a ship owner for an advisor of Job. Even ships are so titled: the *Jeroboam,* the *Rachel.* The historical *Serapis* might have sprung from the same fancy, for to Melville the white-sailed naval vessels, like the albatross, the whale, the skyhawk, were nothing less than archangelic beings. . . .

[Melville's] characters . . . wrestle with problems which have preoccupied heroes, sages, prophets, and gods. They seek the truth in exile and loneliness, in the wilderness of Ishmael and Hagar, of Moses, of John and Jesus. They pursue the demonic phantom despite testimonies of Faust and Prometheus and Jeremiah that they cannot survive the experience. Some announce with Solomon and with Seneca that the wisdom of this world is equivocal, while others, like Enceladus, Hamlet, Jesus, seek to reconcile it with the wisdom of another, absolute realm. At least one meets disaster through the simple opposition of his nature to evil. . . .

LANGUAGE

The speech of these people, too, is appropriate, containing some of the most magnificent of stylistic echoes from the seventeenth century, the Elizabethans, the Anglo-Saxons, the authors of the Bible. The quotations Ishmael makes from

JONAH AS A PREVIEW FOR AHAB

In Moby Dick, *Father Mapple gives a sermon based on the biblical tale of Jonah and the Whale that remarkably echoes what Ishmael will encounter when he meets Ahab and learns of his reasons for hunting the white whale. In this excerpt from the sermon, Father Mapple chides those who, like Jonah, try to shirk their duty to God's requests.*

How being an anointed pilot-prophet, or speaker of true things, and bidden by the Lord to sound those unwelcome truths in the ears of a wicked Nineveh, Jonah, appalled at the hostility he should raise, fled from his mission and sought to escape his duty and his God by taking ship at Joppa. But God is everywhere; Tarshish he never reached. As we have seen, God came upon him in the whale, and swallowed him down to living gulfs of doom, and with swift slantings tore him along 'into the midst of the seas,' where the eddying depths sucked him ten thousand fathoms down, and 'the weeds were wrapped about his head,' and all the watery world of woe bowled over him. Yet even then beyond the reach of any plummet—'out of the belly of hell'—when the whale grounded upon the ocean's utmost bones, even then, God heard the engulphed, repenting prophet when he cried. Then God spake unto the fish; and from the shuddering cold and blackness of the sea, the whale came breeching up towards the warm and pleasant sun, and all the delights of air and earth; and 'vomited out Jonah upon the dry land;' when the word of the Lord came a second thee; and Jonah, bruised and beaten—his ears, like two sea-shells; still multitudinously murmuring of the ocean—Jonah did the Almighty's bidding. And what was that, shipmates? To preach the Truth to the face of Falsehood! That was it!

"This, shipmates, this is that other lesson; and woe to that pilot of the living God who sights it. Woe to him whom this world charms from Gospel duty! Woe to him who seeks to pour oil upon the waters when God has brewed them into a gale! Woe to him who seeks to please rather than to appal! Woe to him whose good name is more to him than goodness! Woe to him who, in this world, courts not dishonor! Woe to him who would not be true, even though to be false were salvation! Yea, woe to him who, as the great Pilot Paul has it, while preaching to others is himself a castaway!"

Job, Father Mapple's sermon on Jonah, the Confidence-Man's reading from Ecclesiasticus, Pierre's relation of the adulteress's story, Nehemiah's recapitulation of obscure biblical events, countless echoes of the Hebrew prophets, poets, and sages—all add eloquence to pretentiousness. Like the Teutonic war song of Yoomy and the Shakespearean ranting of Pierre, these words, whether spoken by or about Melville's characters, make each of them seem less and less like a single individual, more and more like Everyman.

It is in just this conception of character, in fact, that the intricate connections between Melville's religious thought, his use of the Bible, and the entire Romantic school to which he belonged are most clearly revealed. Quite likely its belief in the dignity and the possibility of the individual more than all else commended Christianity to him. For this he held to be the great value, the field on which all conflicts were fought, the divinity shaping every end. Man, by the very fact of his being, could be neither common nor insignificant, and often the darkest of skin and the most primitive of mind held closest communion with the heart of the universe. . . .

All Melville's characters have something in common with the Renaissance and with the Byronic hero. And hence all those in the Bible on whom he depended most to magnify his own were carefully chosen: the ambitious Ahab rather than the repentant David, the rebellious Jonah and the lonely Jeremiah rather than the priestly Isaiah, the aspiring but not the obedient Jesus. For all this is more than magnitude; this is the assault upon the bastions of heaven.

Nor do these characters come alone to Melville's pages. The ancient past to which most of them belong, and which inevitably accompanies them, towers up everywhere, a presence of which he was constantly aware. And again, since none of the scenes of his narratives is older than the eighteenth century, it is largely a figurative method he adopted. The whalemen live together like some old Mesopotamian family. No dying Chaldee had higher or holier thoughts than Queequeg approaching death. Nantucket is the Tyre of New Bedford's Carthage. [In *Pierre*,] the pines on the hill are as "lofty archers, and vast, out-looking watchers of the glorious Babylonian City of the Day." Of the civilizations of Egypt and Assyria, whose secrets were just being excavated, he was particularly fond. . . .

BIBLICAL EPISODES

With such intimations . . . the Bible, of course, abounds; and Melville exploited certain episodes thoroughly: the Creation, the Garden of Eden, the Flood. Sometimes the extent of time is suggested, as when Ishmael is brooding over the dead in the Whaleman's Chapel: "... in what eternal, unstirring paralysis, and deadly, hopeless trance, yet lies antique Adam who died sixty round centuries ago...." Again the emphasis is upon the youthfulness of the world at the time of creation. Exclaimed the champion of contemporary authors, in "Hawthorne and His Mosses": "The world is young to-day as when it was created; and this Vermont morning dew is as wet to my feet as Eden's dew to Adam's."

These allusions are the major part of Melville's effort at "oldageifying youth in books," re-creating as they do an ancient background for his narratives. But he also selected certain strategic points in those narratives to "oldageify" and thereby made them discourses upon themes as old as history....

So in his first novels, wherein Melville compared the life of the Pacific islanders with the life in Eden before the fall, and in his last, which broaches the doctrine of original sin to explain Claggart's character, the entire sequence of events is thrown backward to the beginning of time. The men of the *Pequod* are engaged in no new business: their vessel bears the name of an Indian tribe as extinct as the Medes and the Persians, and the whales they secure contain the stone spearheads of ancient Indian seamen. As Ishmael puts it: "Who can show a pedigree like Leviathan: Ahab's harpoon had shed blood older than the Pharoah's. Methuselah seems a schoolboy. I look round to shake hands with Shem." Nor does the youthful Pierre confront a new problem: it is older than the Glendinning genealogy, older even than Memnon, Solomon, or the Titans, as old as the inscrutable stones of nature. *Clarel*, too, is an old story. Wherever the pilgrims go they are met by memorials of the first century and of the dateless ages preceding it....

For the past he saw was not a separate segment of time but an inextricable part of the present, of which the ruins strewn upon the earth are but the most obvious evidence. From them each succeeding age is built, for time, as he consistently personified it, is the mason, not the destroyer. It sets one generation's life upon its predecessor's, as it did for both Hebrews and Greeks: Ahab's upon Jeroboam's, Orestes' upon Clytemnestra's, Pierre's upon Mr. Glendinning's....

MELVILLE'S USE OF BIBLICAL HEROES

Dreams and portents, hypersensitive natures, and miraculous events—these outline Melville's invisible world. Most of them are described with some reference to supernatural phenomena recorded by history and many in terms of Biblical parallels. The visions of Babbalanja and of Pierre have Hebrew, Miltonic, and Greek echoes; clairvoyants such as Tistig, Elijah, Gabriel, the Manxman, the Dansker resemble and even bear the names of Jewish angels and prophets; spectacles of nature, like the whale's peaking its flukes, are in a class with the activities of Dante's devils and Isaiah's angelic beings; occurrences like Macey's death and the *Pequod's* disaster seem to be the fulfillment of prophecies as divinely inspired as Zoroaster's or as John's. Seeing the dead Claggart lying before him Captain Vere exclaims: "'It is the divine judgment of Ananias! Look!... Struck dead by an angel of God. Yet the angel must hang!'"

Like the past and the present in Melville's pages, moreover, these two spheres of existence are not mutually exclusive, but constantly impinge on each other. They are synchronized. And as natural circumstances are deliberately compared with supernatural ones, a whole undercurrent of affairs is set in motion. Watching Starbuck visit the sleeping Ahab in his cabin and move to slay him with the musket at hand, one suddenly perceives another sequence of events happening at the same moment in quite another world when the mate is said to be wrestling with an angel. These are no theatrical figures of speech; these are glimpses of a realm more dynamic than any other.

Now in his belief in the existence of this world beyond the world of sense Melville has often been called, and even called himself, Platonic. Like the Platonists, he did believe truth resided in the unseen world of ideas and conceptions rather than in the world of material manifestations. But in his essentially romantic conception of this invisible sphere he was closer to the Hebrews than to the Greeks. Order, rhetoric, and logic did not represent the primal truth to him as did elemental and undisciplined energy....

As the sea and the land thus alternate as symbols in his scenes, so the calm and the storm alternate on Melville's sea. For though calmness is sweet and agreeable, the motionless ship is destined to decay. In the rack of the storm it leaps forward, drawing fire from heaven, approaching its goal according as it courts disaster. At the heart of the storm, in the midst of the Great Mutiny, Melville's seekers of truth find and worship it.

This is all in the great tragic tradition of the Hebrews, who regarded the creation, for all its mystery and terror, as the garment of Jehovah. . . .

GOD'S DARK SIDE

It was with something of the primitive spirit of the Hebrews that Melville, too, was more inspired by this manifestation of greatness than of simple goodness. Many were the passages he marked in his Bible illustrating the unequaled and often curiously demonstrated power of Jehovah: his use of Necho the Egyptian to slay Josiah and of Assyria to destroy Samaria. Many were the verses he checked describing Jehovah's darker designs: ". . . for who can make that straight, which he hath made crooked ?" [Eccles. 7:13] ". . . for it must needs be that offences come; but woe to that man by whom the offence cometh!" [Matt. 18:7] "He made darkness his secret place; his pavilion round about him were dark waters and thick clouds of the skies." [Ps. 18:11]

The picture which emerges from all these suggestions, while hardly that which Melville was made acquainted with in the orthodox circles of his youth, is nevertheless one which must have been closer to his heart. Nothing less than a spirit touching good and evil was adequate to preside over the universe he envisaged. Even in his earliest voyages he found that the green valley of the Typee was, like the Garden of Eden, but a small plot of the earth. And to the end, side by side in the Maldive sea, swam the pilot fish and the white shark, as long before the white whale swam ahead of Ahab while the beckoning breezes blew softly from the green shore. The law which could hang a criminal could also hang the purest of the pure, and that without shattering the universe, but only dyeing its vast sky a deeper rose. . . .

It is significant that Melville's persistent image for truth, too, is of something hidden. Ultimate reality exists at the core of this complex universe, at the very heart of its vast reaches, indeed well-nigh impossible to attain for the superficies which surround it. Like Donjalolo [in *Mardi*] "universe-rounded, zodiac-belted, horizon-zoned, sea-girt, reef-sashed, mountain-locked, arbour-nested, royalty-girdled, arm-clasped, self-hugged, indivisible," it dwells at the center of many circumferences. It is a face behind a mask. It is a mummy wrapped in cerements. It is a kernel within a husk. It is deep within a subterranean tunnel. It is at the bottom of a spiral stair. . . .

So all Melville's art and all the vast scene it reared are not ends in themselves but means to an end. All his borrowings and all his conjurings are but approximations. They are circumferences of the center, cerements around the mummy, antechambers to the throne room, husks about the kernel. Not truth itself is his culminating vision, but "cunning glimpses," "occasional flashings-forth," "short, quick probings at the very axis of reality"; symbolic and fragmentary manifestations of the one absolute, which is in the last analysis inviolable.

The Civil War Made Melville a Poet

Robert Penn Warren

Named America's poet laureate in 1986, Robert Penn Warren was a three-time recipient of the Pulitzer Prize, both as a poet and as a novelist. His best-known novel, *All the King's Men*, won the Pulitzer for fiction in 1946. In the following article, Warren comments on the poetry of Herman Melville. Warren maintains that it took the Civil War to turn Melville into a great poet, one who dealt with complex themes in moving verse.

If we are completely to understand Melville's poetry, we must see it against the backdrop of his defeat as a writer, from which he suffered not only the pangs of disappointment and rejection, but the associated distress of ill health, disturbance of vision, and undoubtedly, since his father, after failure, had died mad, the fear of madness. He had reached the hour which he had described in *Pierre*, the time when a man "learns that in his obscurity and indigence humanity holds him a dog and no man," and even the harder hour "when he learns that in his infinite comparative minuteness and abjectness, the gods do likewise despise him." We must see Melville's poetry, too, against the backdrop of grim fortitude and sporadic gaiety, perhaps even grimmer, with which he met the failure; for he clung to the thought, again expressed in *Pierre*, that only after man has passed the hour of total rejection may his soul be "born from the world-husk" and learn to "stand independent.". . .

Part of the effort Melville made to master his fate, and himself, was a trip, in 1856, on the charity of his father-in-law, to Europe and the Holy Land. The family presumably saw travel merely as a distraction from overwork and self-absorbed brooding, and the trip most likely did benefit Mel-

From the Introduction to *Selected Poems of Herman Melville: A Reader's Edition*, edited, with an introduction, by Robert Penn Warren (New York: Random House, 1970). Copyright ©1967, 1970 by Robert Penn Warren. Reprinted by permission of the William Morris Agency, Inc., on behalf of the author.

ville in such obvious commonsensical ways. In his ill-starred venture on the lecture platform two of his offerings were to be "Roman Statuary" and "Traveling, Its Pleasures, Pains, and Profits." But Melville sought more than subjects for lectures; in the journey to the Holy Land Melville saw, or came to see, a symbolic import. He was a seeker of ultimates, a hater of illusion. On his way to the Holy Land, Melville had his last encounter with the admired Hawthorne, who, according to Melville, had had the courage to repudiate all easy solutions to the tragic problem of life. Now on the dunes of Southport, a watering place near Liverpool, where Hawthorne was consul, they talked of the great questions. In his journal Hawthorne reports the occasion:

> Melville, as he always does, began to reason of Providence and futurity, and of everything that lies beyond human ken, and informed me that he had "pretty much made up his mind to be annihilated"; but still he does not seem to rest in the anticipation; and I think, will never rest until he gets hold of a definite belief.

Melville had touched bottom, and he was now seeking a belief by which life could be considered and his own life rebuilt; and his poetry, in one dimension, may be read as a record of that search. . . .

BATTLE-PIECES

The first volume of poems which Melville published was *Battle-Pieces and Aspects of the War*, which appeared in 1866. It is, in many ways, a very remarkable document in the history of American poetry, and a remarkable commentary on the moment in American history. It is also to be remarked in the personal history of the author. War, despite suffering and horror, fulfills certain deep-seated needs in men, affords certain releases, offers certain compensations. Men yearn for significance in life, for the thrill of meaning in action, for communion in a common cause, for the test of their fiber, paradoxically for both the affirmation of, and the death of, the self. Even Hawthorne, despite a premature sense of age, a bleak awareness of the loss of his life-sense and of his creative force, and a peculiarly detached and ironical view of the conflict, could say that the Civil War had a "beneficial effect upon my spirits," and that "it was delightful to share in the heroic sentiment of the time, and to feel that I had a country—a consciousness which seemed to make me young again.". . .

A POET'S SUBJECT

In a very profound way it can be said that the Civil War made Melville a poet. It gave him the right "subject"; and for him the right subject, in prose or poetry, was absolutely essential. For all Melville's metaphysical passion and thirst for ultimates, his creative mind could work only from the stimulation of the concrete, the specific. I do not mean this merely in the sense that all poets, to be poets at all, must be concerned with the physicality of the world. Melville had, in a very special way, a mind that could be truly stirred, be fully engaged, only by what was urgently human, and such a subject had to be come upon in life, had to be torn from actual life, with the raw validation of life.

The Civil War gave Melville the kind of big, athletic, over-mastering subject which he always needed for his best work, and it was bloodily certified by actuality. But there was a paradox in Melville's appetite for the violent subject; such a subject would serve his need only if the centrifugal whirl toward violent action was perfectly balanced by the centripetal pull toward an inwardness of apparently unresolvable mystery, or tormenting ambiguity. Of such inward issues, this outwardly and violently overmastering subject of the Civil War offered God's—and the devil's—plenty.

This complexity in the subject itself—or, rather, the complexity that Melville saw in the subject—had a deep psychological consistency with the kind of style toward which he had been groping in the recent poems. Now, in *Battle-Pieces*, he achieves his best things not by directly imitating the English Metaphysical poets, but by aiming, however uncertainly, at what we may think of as a metaphysical style of his own, which, though vastly different in effect from that of the English poets of the seventeenth century, shared with their style certain assumptions, and even certain methods. He was aiming at a style rich and yet shot through with realism and prosaism, sometimes casual and open and sometimes dense and intellectually weighted, fluid and various because following the contours of his subject, or rather the contours of his complex feelings about his subject. . . .

"THE MARCH INTO VIRGINIA"

Few of Melville's poems are as good, as deeply coherent, as "The March into Virginia," but some of the principles of its

THE MALDIVE SHARK

*Perhaps Melville's best-known poem, "The Maldive Shark"
encompasses the themes to which the author continually returned. Melville comments on both the natural phenomenon
of the habit of pilot fish to swim unharmed around a shark,
and the terrible shark itself.*

About the Shark, phlegmatical one,
Pale sot of the Maldive sea,
The sleek little pilot-fish, azure and slim,
How alert in attendance be.
From his saw-pit of mouth, from his charnel of maw
They have nothing of harm to dread,
But liquidly glide on his ghastly flank
Or before his Gorgonian head;
Or lurk in the port of serrated teeth
In white triple tiers of glittering gates,
And there find a haven when peril's abroad,
An asylum in jaws of the Fates!
They are friends; and friendly they guide him to prey,
Yet never partake of the treat—
Eyes and brains to the dotard lethargic and dull,
Pale ravener of horrible meat.

style do appear rather generally. For example, the use of precise, realistic detail, which was outside the prevailing practice. But not merely the fact of such detail deserves comment; what merits more emphasis is the way in which such
prosaic materials are played against the more conventional
poetic elements. This contrast occurs at the level of mere vocabulary, for Melville, as Newton Arvin has pointed out in
his biography, was given to poeticisms like *fain, deem,* and
wight; technical terms like *caloric, integral, fraction, escheat,
foreclosure*; and coined words like *rugged* (covered as with a
rug), *vowelled, sliddery* (as in the sliddery ledges of ice in
"The Berg").

Vocabulary is, however, only a starting point for such contrasts. For instance, take the first stanza of "Malvern Hill":

Ye elms that wave on Malvern Hill
    In prime of morn and May,
Recall ye how McClellan's men
    Here stood at bay?
While deep within yon forest dim
    Our rigid comrades lay—
Some with the cartridge in their mouth,

Others with fixed arms lifted South—
  Invoking so
The cypress glades? Ah wilds of woe!

The cartridge clenched in the teeth of a dead man, held there as he prepared for loading, suddenly vivifies the stanza. And we may note, too, how the flattened rhythm of the line strikes across the lyricism of the rest.

The whole of "The Armies of the Wilderness" is based on a system of counterpointing; and one of the elements counterpointed is the sort of realism indicated above. The Federal soldiers look across with a telescope to see a "baseball bounding sent," and would like to join the game. Or:

By the bubbling spring lies the rusted canteen,
And the drum which the drummer-boy dying let go.

Or:

The wagon mired and cannon dragged
  Have trenched their scar. . . .

Long sections of realistic dialogue mark the poem; for instance, these lines spoken by a Confederate prisoner being interrogated by his captors as they overlook the Confederate camp:

". . . on the crest,
The Carolinians; lower, past the glen,
Virginians—Alabamians—Mississippians—Kentuckians
  (Follow my finger)—Tennesseans; and the ten
Camps *there*—ask your grave-pits; they'll tell.
  Halloa! I see the picket-hut, the den
Where I last night lay."

Over against such passages we find a lyricism like:

Where are the birds and boys?
Who shall go chestnutting when
October returns? The nuts——
  O, long ere they grow again.

Such stylistic contrasts are most obvious, of course, when occurring within a single poem, but the principle sometimes appears in the juxtaposition of separate pieces. There are poems like the elaborately lyrical "Shiloh" and poems as scrupulously prosaic, except for rhyme, as "Running the Batteries." The most clearly marked instance of stylistic contrast among poems themselves is in the pairing of two poems suggested by the fight between the *Monitor* and the *Merrimac*—the requiem for the "fighting Temeraire," supposed to be spoken by "an Englishman of the old order," and "A Utilitarian View of the Monitor's Fight." The first poem ends:

> But Fame has nailed your battle-flags—
> Your ghost it sails before:
> O, the navies old and oaken,
> O, the Temeraire no morel

The second poem begins, "Plain be the phrase," and the plainness of phrase is part, as it were, of the subject matter of the poem—of "The clangor of that blacksmiths' fray," in which

> . . . all went on by crank,
> Pivot, and screw,
> And calculations of caloric.

The poem ends with a brilliant metaphor which snatches the poem from the jaws of prose:

> War shall yet be, and to the end;
> But war-paint shows the streaks of weather;
> War yet shall be, but warriors
> Are now operatives; War's made
> Less grand than Peace,
> And a singe runs through lace and feather.

The poem itself states, as well as illustrates, the assumptions behind Melville's style: a world in which a singe runs through lace and feather demands an appropriate style.

THE END OF ILLUSION

Melville saw, however, another kind of singe running through the lace and feather of life. Every man must confront it, sooner or later, the painful end of illusion, the dire destiny of the passage round the Horn, just as America was confronting it in the Civil War. But not only in the moment of great crisis is there the "singe": in the ordinary course of life, there is a doubleness in things. If Nature seems beneficent and beautiful, that is only one aspect, for, as it is put in "Misgivings," there is "Nature's darker side," and as, in "The Stone Fleet," the sailor says, "Nature is nobody's ally."

Such doubleness lies in history, too. Man is doomed to exert will to control events, but even when he seems to act effectively, the process in which his will operates may be only a mask for a secret process of which he has suspected nothing. So we find it said in "Misgivings," in which, as of 1860, the poet broods on the impending conflict:

> And storms are formed behind the storm we feel:
> The hemlock shakes in the rafter, the oak in the driving
> keel.

And in "The Conflict of Convictions," the wind of History "spins *against* the way it drives." For example, by the victory of "Right" in the Civil War, certain undreamed-of forces may be released so that

> Power unanointed may come—
> Dominion (unsought by the free)
>   And the Iron Dome,
> Stronger for stress and strain,
> Fling her huge shadow athwart the main;
> But the Founders' dream shall flee.

But there are other polarities and ambiguities in life. A decision presumably made on idealistic grounds may simply be the reflex of a historical situation. "On the Slain Collegians" shows young men of both North and South "swept by the wind of their place and time." Even if an ethical distinction is to be made at the level of the cause for which war is being waged, at another level such a distinction is irrelevant:

> Warred one for Right, and one for Wrong?
> So be it; but they both were young—
> Each grape to his cluster clung,
> All their elegies are sung.

Each was doomed to cling to his cluster, and in this fact is implicit the polarity of "ideology" ("Law," "Right," or even "Destiny") against human values, human suffering, human aspiration, qualities of personality and spirit.

The human bond may be as important as the bond of ideology. As "On the Photograph of a Corps Commander" puts it:

> Nothing can lift the heart of man
> Like manhood in a fellow-man.

And the fellow-man may be a fellow, not by ideology but only in his manhood. Stonewall Jackson and Lee are noble enemies, are nobly wrong. In "Donelson," we find that the "Rebel," though he is in the wrong, defends "a perverted Bunker Hill." A recognition of the human community is an essential virtue, and the human community is, in one perspective, a community of guilt, as we find in "The Swamp Angel," the poem on the bombardment of Charleston, South Carolina:

> Who weeps for the woeful City
>   Let him weep for our guilty kind;
> Who joys at her wild despairing—
>   Christ, the Forgiver, convert his mind.

A recognition of the human as distinguished from the ideological makes magnanimity possible, and Melville ends the volume with a poem called "A Meditation," and the lines:

> When Vicksburg fell, and the moody files marched out,
> Silent the victors stood, scorning to raise a shout.

"Man honors man" beyond "cause," as Melville says in "Magnanimity Baffled," knowing, if he is wise, that even the best cause does violence to some values, and that, as William James remarks in "Pragmatism and Religion," after victory "something apparently drastic and bitter always remains in the bottom of the cup."

THE FACT OF DEATH

The most painful polarity of all is that between all values and the blank fact of annihilation. As in "Sheridan at Cedar Creek,"

> There is glory for the brave
> Who lead, and nobly save,
> But no knowledge in the grave
> Where the nameless followers sleep.

But the same fact of annihilation—the subject on which Melville had brooded so much—which appears in this poem as mere blankness may elsewhere be regarded as a peace, with the problem of values in the flux of history resolved, however perilously and equivocally, in the context of natural process. For instance, in "Malvern Hill," the elms remember the horror and heroism of the battle,

> *But sap the twig will fill:*
> *Wag the world how it will,*
> *Leaves must be green in Spring.*

But if death is blankness—or even blankness regarded as elegiac peace—how can values be found in action desperately foredoomed to blankness? The answer is by a stoicism at once self-assertive and self-denying. It is self-assertive in the courage to endure, and by endurance to define its own value, outside of time, as in the poem on the prisoners who died at Andersonville, in Georgia, "On a Natural Monument":

> Their fame is this: they did endure—
> Endure, when fortitude was vain
> To kindle any approving strain
> Which they might hear. To these who rest
> This healing sleep alone was sure.

But stoicism may be self-denying in the will to sink the personal pain in a compassionate and ennobling awareness of the general human lot, as in another poem on a forgotten monument, "An Uninscribed Monument":

> Thou who beholdest, if thy thought,
> Not narrowed down to personal cheer,
> Take in the import of the quiet here—
>   The after-quiet—the calm full fraught;
> Thou too wilt silent stand—
> Silent as I, and lonesome as the land.

There is, however, another way of regarding action, another polarity involving it. The act is in time. It is at the knife-edge moment of the present, between the past and the future, and at this moment it both projects and fulfills life. But as the life projected into the future is fulfilled, the act with all its urgencies disappears into the past. Action becomes legend.

This theme is continually implicit in *Battle-Pieces*, but its fullest poetic embodiment is in "Battle of Stone River, Tennessee," which is described in the subtitle as "A View from Oxford Cloisters." Here, half a world away from the battle, a learned don might ironically convert his distance in space into a distance in time, and muse that the present conflict, with all its issues and urgencies, will soon be no more for America than the War of the Roses is for England: "In legend all shall end."

In the very moment of action, action enters into legend:

> But Rosecrans in the cedarn glade,
>   And, deep in denser cypress gloom,
> Dark Breckinridge, shall fade away
>   Or thinly loom.
> The pale throngs who in forest cowed
>   Before the spell of battle's pause,
> Forefelt the stillness that shall dwell
>   On them and on their wars.
>   North and South shall join the train
>   Of Yorkist and Lancastrian.

TRAGIC INSIGHT

... The underlying tragic insight of *Battle-Pieces* is ... the necessity for action in the face of the difficulty of knowing truth. In this situation man becomes fully man only if he submits himself to the complications of the inwardness of life in order to be returned, chastened and enlightened, to the objective world of action. In this case—the case of the Civil War—Melville, speaking for and to the victors, holds that the chastening would lie in the discovery of the victorious *self* as blood kin, in the human plight of virtue-in-guilt and guilt-in-virtue, to the defeated *other*, and that this enlightenment would, in the end, be Melville's way of trying to follow the prescription of William James for doing "justice to the ideals in which the vanquished interests lay.". . .

A FAILURE

When *Battle-Pieces* appeared, Melville had been desperately in need of money as well as appreciation; and with a book on such a topic, and in a period when a volume of poetry not infrequently sold like a popular novel today, Melville's hope, a hope that today would mark a poet as a certifiable lunatic, had some grounding in reality. With this hope blasted, Melville faced the brute fact that he could make neither a living nor a name, by his pen. He had failed, too, in his hope to convert his guttering fame into a competence by means of a consular appointment. He was now ready to descend into his Tartarus, the Customs House of the Port of New York, where he became an inspector—an occupation which, years before, in *Redburn*, he had described as more inglorious than "driving geese to water." So now, at the age of forty-seven, at the wage of four dollars a day, Melville made his terms with the world, and with fate.

CHAPTER 2

A Critical Selection

READINGS ON
HERMAN MELVILLE

Typee and Omoo: Melville's Contemplation of Paradise

D.H. Lawrence

In this unique essay excerpted from D.H. Lawrence's collected literary criticism, *Studies in Classic American Literature*, novelist Lawrence critiques Melville's successful early novels *Typee* and *Omoo*. Lawrence claims that Melville proves a bitter truth: No matter how much humanity yearns to return to the time of Eden, it cannot. Modern humans cannot coexist in a paradisical environment, argues Lawrence, that ultimately produces childlike and irresponsible adults. English novelist D.H. Lawrence's most famous works include *Lady Chatterley's Lover*, *Women in Love*, and *The Plumed Serpent*.

The greatest seer and poet of the sea for me is Melville. His vision is more real than Swinburne's, because he doesn't personify the sea, and far sounder than Joseph Conrad's, because Melville doesn't sentimentalize the ocean and the sea's unfortunates. Snivel in a wet hanky like Lord Jim.

Melville has the strange, uncanny magic of sea-creatures, and some of their repulsiveness. He isn't quite a land animal. There is something slithery about him. Something always half-seas-over. In his life they said he was mad—or crazy. He was neither mad nor crazy. But he was over the border. He was half a water animal, like those terrible yellow-bearded Vikings who broke out of the waves in beaked ships. . . .

Melville was a northerner, sea-born. So the sea claimed him. We are most of us, who use the English language, water-people, sea-derived.

Melville went back to the oldest of all the oceans, to the Pacific. . . .

Without doubt the Pacific Ocean is aeons older than the Atlantic or the Indian Oceans. When we say older, we mean it has not come to any modern consciousness. Strange convulsions have convulsed the Atlantic and Mediterranean peoples into phase after phase of consciousness, while the Pacific and the Pacific peoples have slept. To sleep is to dream: you can't stay unconscious. And, oh heaven, for how many thousands of years has the true Pacific been dreaming, turning over in its sleep and dreaming again: idylls: nightmares.

The Maoris, the Tongans, the Marquesans, the Fijians, the Polynesians: holy God, how long have they been turning over in the same sleep, with varying dreams? Perhaps, to a sensitive imagination, those islands in the middle of the Pacific are the most unbearable places on earth. It simply stops the heart, to be translated there, unknown ages back, back into that life, that pulse, that rhythm. The scientists say the South Sea Islanders belong to the Stone Age. It seems absurd to class people according to their implements. And yet there is something in it. The heart of the Pacific is still the Stone Age; in spite of steamers. The heart of the Pacific seems like a vast vacuum, in which, mirage-like, continues the life of myriads of ages back. It is a phantom-persistence of human beings who should have died, by our chronology, in the Stone Age. It is a phantom, illusion-like trick of reality: the glamorous South Seas. . . .

To this phantom, Melville returned. Back, back, away from life. Never man instinctively hated human life, our human life, as we have it, more than Melville did. And never was a man so passionately filled with the sense of vastness and mystery of life which is non-human. He was mad to look over our horizons. Anywhere, anywhere out of *our* world. To get away. To get away, out!

TO ANOTHER LIFE

To get away, out of our life. To cross a horizon into another life. No matter what life, so long as it is another life.

Away, away from humanity. To the sea. The naked salt, elemental sea. To go to sea, to escape humanity.

The human heart gets into a frenzy at last, in its desire to dehumanize itself.

So he finds himself in the middle of the Pacific. Truly over a horizon. In another world. In another epoch. Back, far back, in the days of palm trees and lizards and stone implements. The sunny Stone Age.

Samoa, Tahiti, Raratonga, Nukuheva: the very names are a sleep and a forgetting. The sleep-forgotten past magnificence of human history. "Trailing clouds of glory."

Melville hated the world: was born hating it. But he was looking for heaven. That is, choosingly. Choosingly, he was looking for paradise. Unchoosingly, he was mad with hatred of the world.

Well, the world is hateful. It is as hateful as Melville found it. He was not wrong in hating the world. . . . He hated it to a pitch of madness, and not without reason.

But it's no good *persisting* in looking for paradise "regained."

Melville at his best invariably wrote from a sort of dream-self, so that events which he relates as actual fact have indeed a far deeper reference to his own soul, his own inner life.

So in *Typee* when he tells of his entry into the valley of the dread cannibals of Nukuheva. Down this narrow, steep, horrible dark gorge he slides and struggles as we struggle in a dream, or in the act of birth, to emerge in the green Eden of the Golden Age, the valley of the cannibal savages. This is a bit of birth-myth, or re-birth myth, on Melville's part—unconscious, no doubt, because his running underconsciousness was always mystical and symbolical. He wasn't aware that he was being mystical.

There he is then, in Typee, among the dreaded cannibal savages. And they are gentle and generous with him, and he is truly in a sort of Eden.

Here at last is Rousseau's Child of Nature and Chateaubriand's Noble Savage called upon and found at home. Yes, Melville loves his savage hosts. He finds them gentle, laughing lambs compared to the ravening wolves of his white brothers, left behind in America and on an American whaleship.

The ugliest beast on earth is the white man, says Melville.

In short, Herman found in Typee the paradise he was looking for. It is true, the Marquesans were "immoral," but he rather liked that. Morality was too white a trick to take him in. Then again, they were cannibals. And it filled him with horror even to think of this. But the savages were very private and even fiercely reserved in their cannibalism, and he might have spared himself his shudder. No doubt he had partaken of the Christian Sacraments many a time. "This is my body, take and eat. This is my blood. Drink it in remembrance of me." And if the savages liked to partake of their sacrament without raising the transubstantiation quibble, and if they liked to say, directly: "This is thy body, which I take from thee and eat. This is thy blood, which I sip in annihilation of thee," why surely their sacred ceremony was as awe-inspiring as the one Jesus substituted. But Herman chose to be horrified. I confess, I am not horrified; though, of course, I am not on the spot. But the savage sacrament seems to me more valid than the Christian: less side-tracking about it. Thirdly, he was shocked by their wild methods of warfare. He died before the great European war, so his shock was comfortable.

Three little quibbles: morality, cannibal sacrament, and stone axes. You must have a fly even in Paradisal ointment. And the first was a ladybird.

Unhappy in Paradise

But Paradise. He insists on it. Paradise. He could even go stark naked, as before the Apple episode. And his Fayaway, a laughing little Eve, naked with him, and hankering after no apple of knowledge, so long as he would just love her when he felt like it. Plenty to eat, needing no clothes to wear, sunny, happy people, sweet water to swim in: everything a man can want. Then why wasn't he happy along with the savages?

Because he wasn't.

He grizzled in secret, and wanted to escape.

He even pined for Home and Mother, the two things he had run away from as far as ships would carry him. HOME and MOTHER. The two things that were his damnation.

There on the island, where the golden-green great palmtrees chinked in the sun, and the elegant reed houses let the sea-breeze through, and people went naked and laughed a great deal, and Fayaway put flowers in his hair for him—great red hibiscus flowers, and frangipani—O God, why wasn't he happy? Why wasn't he?

Because he wasn't.

Well, it's hard to make a man happy.

But I should not have been happy either. One's soul seems under a vacuum, in the South Seas.

The truth of the matter is, one cannot go back. Some men can: renegade. But Melville couldn't go back: and Gauguin couldn't really go back: and I know now that I could never go back. Back towards the past, savage life. One cannot go back. It is one's destiny inside one.

There are these peoples, these "savages." One does not despise them. One does not feel superior. But there is a gulf. There is a gulf in time and being. I cannot commingle my being with theirs.

There they are, these South Sea Islanders, beautiful big men with their golden limbs and their laughing, graceful laziness. And they will call you brother, choose you as a brother. But why cannot one truly be brother?

There is an invisible hand grasps my heart and prevents it opening too much to these strangers. They are beautiful, they are like children, they are generous: but they are more than this. They are far off, and in their eyes is an easy darkness of the soft, uncreate past. In a way, they are uncreate. Far be it from me to assume any "white" superiority. But they are savages. They are gentle and laughing and physically very handsome. But it seems to me, that in living so far, through all our bitter centuries of civilization, we have still been living onwards, forwards. God knows it looks like a *cul de sac* now. But turn to the first negro, and then listen to your own soul. And your own soul will tell you that however false and foul our forms and systems are now, still, through the many centuries since Egypt, we have been living and struggling forwards along some road that is no road, and yet is a great life-development. We have struggled on, and on we must still go. We may have to smash things. Then let us smash. And our road may have to take a great swerve, that seems a retrogression.

But we can't go back. Whatever else the South Sea Islander is, he is centuries and centuries behind us in the life-struggle, the consciousness-struggle, the struggle of the soul into fulness. There is his woman, with her knotted hair and her dark, inchoate, slightly sardonic eyes. I like her, she is nice. But I would never want to touch her. I could not go back on myself so far. Back to their uncreate condition.

She has soft warm flesh, like warm mud. Nearer the reptile, the Saurian age. . . .

WE CAN'T GO BACK TO PARADISE

We can't go back. We can't go back to the savages: not a stride. We can be in sympathy with them. We can take a great curve in their direction, onwards. But we cannot turn the current of our life backwards, back towards their soft warm twilight and uncreate mud. Not for a moment. If we do it for a moment, it makes us sick.

We can only do it when we are renegade. The renegade hates life itself. He wants the death of life. So these many "reformers" and "idealists" who glorify the savages in America. They are death-birds, life-haters. Renegades.

We can't go back, and Melville couldn't. Much as he hated the civilized humanity he knew. He couldn't go back to the savages; he wanted to, he tried to, and he couldn't.

Because, in the first place, it made him sick; it made him physically ill. He had something wrong with his leg, and this would not heal. It got worse and worse, during his four months on the island. When he escaped, he was in a deplorable condition—sick and miserable, ill, very ill.

Paradise!

But there you are. Try to go back to the savages, and you feel as if your very soul was decomposing inside you. That is what you feel in the South Seas, anyhow: as if your soul was decomposing inside you. And with any savages the same, if you try to go their way, take their current of sympathy.

Yet, as I say, we must make a great swerve in our onward-going life-course now, to gather up again the savage mysteries. But this does not mean going back on ourselves.

Going back to the savages made Melville sicker than anything. It made him feel as if he were decomposing. Worse even than Home and Mother.

And that is what really happens. If you prostitute your psyche by returning to the savages, you gradually go to pieces. Before you can go back, you *have* to decompose. And a white man decomposing is a ghastly sight. Even Melville in Typee.

We have to go on, on, on, even if we must smash a way ahead.

So Melville escaped, and threw a boat-hook full in the throat of one of his dearest savage friends, and sank him, because that savage was swimming in pursuit. That's how he felt about the savages when they wanted to detain him. He'd have murdered them one and all, vividly, rather than be kept from escaping. Away from them—he must get away from them—at any price.

And once he has escaped, immediately he begins to sigh

and pine for the "Paradise"—Home and Mother being at the other end even of a whaling voyage.

When he really was Home with Mother, he found it Purgatory. But Typee must have been even worse than Purgatory, a soft hell, judging from the murderous frenzy which possessed him to escape.

But once aboard the whaler that carried him off from Nukuheva, he looked back and sighed for the Paradise he had just escaped from in such a fever.

Poor Melville! He was determined Paradise existed. So he was always in Purgatory.

He was born for Purgatory. Some souls are purgatorial by destiny.

The very freedom of his Typee was a torture to him. Its ease was slowly horrible to him. This time *he* was the fly in the odorous tropical ointment.

He needed to fight. It was no good to him, the relaxation of the nonmoral tropics. He didn't really want Eden. He wanted to fight. Like every American. To fight. But with weapons of the spirit, not the flesh.

That was the top and bottom of it. His soul was in revolt, writhing for ever in revolt. When he had something definite to rebel against—like the bad conditions on a whaling ship—then he was much happier in his miseries. The mills of God were grinding inside him, and they needed something to grind on.

When they could grind on the injustice and folly of missionaries, or of brutal sea-captains, or of governments, he was easier. The mills of God were grinding inside him.

They are grinding inside every American. And they grind exceeding small.

Why? Heaven knows. But we've got to grind down our old forms, our old selves, grind them very very small, to nothingness. Whether a new somethingness will ever start, who knows? Meanwhile the mills of God grind on, in American Melville, and it was himself he ground small: himself and his wife, when he was married. For the present, the South Seas.

He escapes on to the craziest, most impossible of whaling ships. Lucky for us Melville makes it fantastic. It must have been pretty sordid.

And anyhow, on the crazy *Julia*, his leg, that would never heal in the paradise of Typee, began quickly to get well. His life was falling into its normal pulse. The drain back into past centuries was over.

Yet, oh, as he sails away from Nukuheva, on the voyage that will ultimately take him to America, oh, the acute and intolerable nostalgia he feels for the island he has left.

The past, the Golden Age of the past—what a nostalgia we all feel for it. Yet we don't want it when we get it. Try the South Seas.

SEARCHING FOR THE IDEAL

Melville had to fight, fight against the existing world, against his own very self. Only he would never quite put the knife in the heart of his paradisal ideal. Somehow, somewhere, somewhen, love should be a fulfilment, and life should be a thing of bliss. That was his fixed ideal. . . .

That was the pin he tortured himself on, like a pinned-down butterfly.

Love is never a fulfilment. Life is never a thing of continuous bliss. There is no paradise. Fight and laugh and feel bitter and feel bliss: and fight again. Fight, fight. That is life.

Why pin ourselves down on a paradisal ideal? It is only ourselves we torture.

Melville did have one great experience, getting away from humanity: the experience of the sea.

The South Sea Islands were not his great experience. They were a glamorous world outside New England. Outside. But it was the sea that was both outside and inside: the universal experience.

The book that follows on from *Typee* is *Omoo*.

Omoo is a fascinating book; picaresque, rascally, roving. Melville, as a bit of a beachcomber. The crazy ship *Julia* sails to Tahiti, and the mutinous crew are put ashore. Put in the Tahitian prison. It is good reading.

Perhaps Melville is at his best, his happiest, in *Omoo*. For once he is really reckless. For once he takes life as it comes. For once he is the gallant rascally epicurean, eating the world like a snipe, dirt and all baked into one *bonne bouche.*

For once he is really careless, roving with that scamp, Doctor Long Ghost. For once he is careless of his actions, careless of his morals, careless of his ideals: ironic, as the epicurean must be. The deep irony of your real scamp: your real epicurean of the moment.

But it was under the influence of the Long Doctor. This long and bony Scotsman was not a mere ne'er-do-well. He

was a man of humorous desperation, throwing his life ironically away. Not a mere loose-kneed loafer, such as the South
Seas seem to attract.

That is good about Melville: he never repents. Whatever
he did, in Typee or in Doctor Long Ghost's wicked society,
he never repented. If he ate his snipe, dirt and all, and enjoyed it at the time, he didn't have bilious bouts afterwards,
which is good.

But it wasn't enough. The Long Doctor was really knocking about in a sort of despair. He let his ship drift rudderless.

Melville couldn't do this. For a time, yes. For a time, in this
Long Doctor's company, he was rudderless and reckless.
Good as an experience. But a man who will not abandon
himself to despair or indifference cannot keep it up.

Melville would never abandon himself either to despair
or indifference. He always cared. He always cared enough to
hate missionaries, and to be touched by a real act of kindness. He always cared.

When he saw a white man really "gone savage," a white
man with a blue shark tattooed over his brow, gone over to
the savages, then Herman's whole being revolted. He couldn't
bear it. He could not bear a renegade.

He enlisted at last on an American man-of-war. You have
the record in *White-Jacket*. He was back in civilization, but
still at sea. He was in America, yet loose in the seas. Good
regular days, after Doctor Long Ghost and the *Julia.*

BOUND TO CIVILIZATION

As a matter of fact, a long thin chain was round Melville's
ankle all the time, binding him to America, to civilization, to
democracy, to the ideal world. It was a long chain, and it
never broke. It pulled him back.

By the time he was twenty-five his wild oats were sown;
his reckless wanderings were over. At the age of twenty-five
he came back to Home and Mother, to fight it out at close
quarters. For you can't fight it out by running away. When
you have run a long way from Home and Mother, then you
realize that the earth is round, and if you keep on running
you'll be back on the same old doorstep,—like a fatality.

Melville came home to face out the long rest of his life. He
married and had an ecstasy of a courtship and fifty years of
disillusion.

He had just furnished his home with disillusions. No

more Typees. No more paradises. No more Fayaways. A mother: a gorgon. A home: a torture box. A wife: a thing with clay feet. Life: a sort of disgrace. Fame: another disgrace, being patronized by common snobs who just know how to read.

The whole shameful business just making a man writhe.

Melville writhed for eighty years.

In his soul he was proud and savage.

But in his mind and will he wanted the perfect fulfilment of love; he wanted the lovey-doveyness of perfect mutual understanding.

A proud savage-souled man doesn't really want any perfect lovey-dovey fulfilment in love: no such nonsense. A mountain lion doesn't mate with a Persian cat; and when a grizzly bear roars after a mate, it is a she-grizzly he roars after—not after a silky sheep.

But Melville stuck to his ideal. He wrote *Pierre* to show that the more you try to be good the more you make a mess of things: that following righteousness is just disastrous. The better you are, the worse things turn out with you. The better you try to be, the bigger mess you make. Your very striving after righteousness only causes your own slow degeneration.

Well, it is true. No men are so evil to-day as the idealists, and no women half so evil as your earnest woman, who feels herself a power for good. It is inevitable. After a certain point, the ideal goes dead and rotten. The old pure ideal becomes in itself an impure thing of evil. Charity becomes pernicious, the spirit itself becomes foul. The meek are evil. The pure in heart have base, subtle revulsions: like Dostoevsky's Idiot. The whole Sermon on the Mount becomes a litany of white vice.

What then?

It's our own fault. It was *we* who set up the ideals. And if we are such fools, that we aren't able to kick over our ideals in time, the worse for us.

Look at Melville's eighty long years of writhing. And to the end he writhed on the ideal pin.

From the "perfect woman lover" he passed on to the "perfect friend." He looked and looked for the perfect man friend.

Couldn't find him.

Marriage was a ghastly disillusion to him, because he looked for perfect marriage.

Friendship never even made a real start in him—save perhaps his half-sentimental love for Jack Chase, in *White-Jacket.*

Yet to the end he pined for this: a perfect relationship; perfect mating; perfect mutual understanding. A perfect friend.

Right to the end he could never accept the fact that *perfect* relationships cannot be. Each soul is alone, and the aloneness of each soul is a double barrier to perfect relationship between two beings.

Each soul *should* be alone. And in the end the desire for a "perfect relationship" is just a vicious, unmanly craving. . . .

Melville, however, refused to draw his conclusion. *Life* was wrong, he said. He refused Life. But he stuck to his ideal of perfect relationship, possible perfect love. The world *ought* to be a harmonious loving place. And it *can't* be. So life itself is wrong.

It is silly arguing. Because, after all, only temporary man sets up the "oughts."

The world ought *not* to be a harmonious loving place. It ought to be a place of fierce discord and intermittent harmonies: which it is.

Love ought *not* to be perfect. It ought to have perfect moments, and wildernesses of thorn bushes—which it has.

A "perfect" relationship ought *not* to be possible. Every relationship should have its absolute limits, its absolute reserves, essential to the singleness of the soul in each person. A truly perfect relationship is one in which each party leaves great tracts unknown in the other party.

No two persons can meet at more than a few points, consciously. If two people can just be together fairly often, so that the presence of each is a sort of balance to the other, that is the basis of perfect relationship. There must be true separatenesses as well.

Melville was, at the core, a mystic and an idealist.

Perhaps, so am I.

And he stuck to his ideal guns.

I abandon mine.

He was a mystic who raved because the old ideal guns shot havoc. The guns of the "noble spirit." Of "ideal love."

I say, let the old guns rot.

Get new ones, and shoot straight.

Benito Cereno Reveals Melville's Belief in Racial Equality

Edward S. Grejda

Literary critic Edward S. Grejda is the author of *The Common Continent of Men: Racial Equality in the Writings of Herman Melville*. Many critics have puzzled over Melville's dark tale *Benito Cereno*, contending that it stereotypes blacks as savage and uncivilized. In the following article, Grejda argues the opposite. He contends that the tale is about mutual distrust between the races, which, he argues, is inspired by whites' condescending stereotypes of and attitudes toward blacks.

Benito Cereno, Melville's tale of mutiny aboard the Spanish ship *San Dominick* captained by Don Benito Cereno, is a drama in which nonwhites occupy center stage. The story unfolds through the consciousness of a native of Duxbury, Massachusetts, Captain Amasa Delano, who, seeing the *San Dominick* in a shocking state of decay floundering toward a reef, comes to its aid. Once aboard, Delano cannot know what Benito does—that the principal cargo of the vessel, 160 Negro slaves, have mutinied and killed most of the crew. Their leader is the Senegalese Negro Babo, who, disguised as the solicitous body servant of Cereno, has organized every person aboard in an ingenious masquerade to deceive the American captain. Alternating between mistrust and reassurance over the ambiguous actions of Cereno, crew and slaves, but failing to penetrate the true nature of the mystery, Delano's mind makes *Benito Cereno* a masterpiece of suspense, many particulars of which are not known until after the narrative climax. At this point, the specifics of the revolt are revealed through lengthy extracts from the testimony of Benito, who gives his deposition during the trial of the mu-

From *The Common Continent of Men: Racial Equality in the Writings of Herman Melville* by Edward S. Grejda (Port Washington, NY: National University Publications, 1974). Copyright ©1974 by Kennikat Press Corp.

tineers. Suspense, however, is of secondary importance. The fascinating enigma of *Benito Cereno* revolves around the question of what Melville intended his blacks to be. . . .

EVIL AND GOOD ARE BLURRED

Melville's characters in *Benito Cereno* cannot be placed within a strict good-evil framework. White sailors and black slaves, rather than being "whitened" and "blackened," merge into gray, a color which blurs any distinction between them. Interestingly, Melville sets the tone of his tale with an early emphasis on gray:

> Everything was mute and calm; everything gray. The sea, though undulated into long roods of swells, seemed fixed, and was sleeked at the surface like waved lead that has cooled and set in the smelter's mould. The sky seemed a gray surtout. Flights of troubled gray foul, kith and kin with flights of troubled gray vapours among which they were mixed, skimmed low and fitfully over the waters, as swallows over meadows before storms. Shadows present, foreshadowing deeper shadows to come.

In the world of gray shadows, this "smelter's pot," humans cannot be readily dichotomized. Man, as evidenced by the duality (i.e., man-devil, lion-lamb) of many of Melville's earlier characters, may evoke both admiration and revulsion. In this connection, Melville offers a revealing observation in his "Sketch Second" of "The Encantadas":

> Even the tortoise, dark and melancholy as it is upon the back, still possesses a bright side; its calipee or breast-plate being sometimes of a faint yellowish or golden tinge. Moreover, everyone knows that tortoises as well as turtles are of such a make, that if you but put them on their backs you thereby expose their bright sides without the possibility of their recovering themselves, and turning into view the other. But after you have done this, and because you have done this, you should not swear that the tortoise has no dark side. Enjoy the bright, keep it turned up perpetually if you can, but be honest, and don't deny the black. Neither should he, who cannot turn the tortoise from its natural position so as to hide the darker and expose its livelier aspect, like a great October pumpkin in the sun, for that cause declare the creature to be one total inky blot. The tortoise is both black and bright.

Like the tortoise, Babo and the Negroes aboard the *San Dominick* are neither black (pure evil) nor bright (angels avenging a moral wrong). By showing both sides of whites and blacks, by illustrating the universality of the savage impulse, Melville again dramatizes the sameness of man. But, as Melville says in "The Encantadas," "Let us to particulars."

Trusting and benevolent as Captain Delano is, one cannot ignore the possibility of his being an object of satire, what [critic] Charles I. Glicksberg calls "a composite reflection of the righteous stereotyped attitudes prevalent at the time." To the good American captain, "a man of such native simplicity as to be incapable of satire or irony," the Negro is simply not an individual; he takes "humane satisfaction" in seeing the blacks dutifully performing their designated roles in life. He notes the "peculiar love in negroes of uniting industry with pastime," and he is amused by "the African love of bright colours and fine shows." He admires in the Negro servant "that affectionate zeal which transmutes into something filial or fraternal acts in themselves but menial; and which has gained for the negro the repute of making the most pleasing body-servant in the world; one, too, whom a master need be on no stiffly superior terms with, but may treat with familiar trust; less a servant than a devoted companion." To the "blunt thinking" American, the "menial familiarity" of the black servant is marked by the "charm of simple-hearted attachment." That "charm" is also evident in Delano's pastoral view of the female slaves: Negresses are "unsophisticated as leopardesses; loving as doves"; another is "like a doe" and her infant a "wide-awake fawn." In Delano's consciousness no detail of the Negro stereotype is overlooked:

> There is something in the negro which, in a peculiar way, fits him for avocations about one's person. Most negroes are natural valets and hair dressers; taking to the comb and brush congenially as to the castanets, and flourishing them apparently with almost equal satisfaction. There is, too, a smooth tact about them in this employment, with a marvellous, noiseless, gliding briskness, not ungraceful in its way, singularly pleasing to behold, and still more so to be the manipulated subject of. And above all is the great gift of good humour. Not the mere grin or laugh is here meant. Those were unsuitable. But a certain easy cheerfulness, harmonious in every glance and gesture; as though God had set the whole negro to some pleasant tune.

FATAL STEREOTYPES

... Even when a Spanish lad is knifed by a Negro boy and a sailor is trampled by two Negroes, Delano's veil of bias enables him to rationalize. His comfortable assumptions about the Negro character do not allow for the possibility of their being savage; his superficial appraisal does not admit that

Negroes might seek their freedom. After all, "Newfoundland dogs" are domesticated and loyal. . . .

DELANO'S RACISM

Throughout Benito Cereno, *the character of Captain Delano sees many strange and blatant actions by the crew that should tip him off that a mutiny has occurred. Yet, because of his stereotypes of blacks, who are the mutineers, Delano cannot interpret the events correctly. In this excerpt, Delano puzzles over Don Benito's (Benito Cereno's) criticisms of his crew, and again misses the point when he stereotypes the blacks onboard.*

Was it from foreseeing some possible interference . . . that Don Benito had, beforehand, given such a bad character of his sailors, while praising the negroes; though, indeed, the former seemed as docile as the latter the contrary? The whites, too, by nature, were the shrewder race. A man with some evil design, would he not be likely to speak well of that stupidity which was blind to his depravity, and malign that intelligence from which it might not be hidden? Not unlikely, perhaps. If the whites had dark secrets concerning Don Benito, could then Don Benito be any way in complicity with the blacks? But they were too stupid. Besides, who ever heard of a white so far a renegade as to apostatize from his very species almost, by leaguing in against it with negroes?

If Delano's "weakness for Negroes" causes their image to be distorted, what, then, is the reality of the blacks? From the . . . extracts from Cereno's deposition during the trial, we discover that the man whom Delano sees as a solicitous and charming menial is capable of animal savagery. The Negroes murdered "eighteen men of those who were sleeping upon deck, some with handspikes and hatchets, and others by throwing them alive overboard, after tying them." The owner of the slaves, Don Alexandro Aranda, was dragged mangled and half alive to the deck where his murder was completed before the eyes of Babo. His body, stripped of flesh "in a way which [Benito Cereno], so long as reason is left him, can never divulge," was then mounted below the ship's figurehead to remind the other whites of what could be their fate. The Negresses, had they not been restrained, "would have tortured to death, instead of simply killing, the Spaniards slain by command of the negro Babo." From the deposition we also learn "that the negroes broke an arm of one of the cabin-boys and gave him strokes with hatchets." Another Spaniard had hot tar poured over his hands. Still others, their arms bound, were thrown alive into the sea. Of the thirty-six crewmen, only six remained alive. In this document of horror, Delano's Newfoundland dogs become wolves....

It is not surprising, then, that many readers, repelled by the Negro atrocities and by the animal images, view the blacks as a malignant, destructive force and, accordingly, empathize with the helpless, victimized whites. In a sense, such readers have greater perception than Delano; whereas he acknowledges neither the man nor the beast, they see at least the beast. The man, however, is also there.

The Negroes in *Benito Cereno* are neither Delano's docile subservients nor ravenous animals. Both assessments represent an extreme, an indictment of an entire race by a man whose concern lies with the "common continent of men." As with the Galapagos tortoise, Melville has not denied the dark side of the Negroes. But neither are they "one total inky blot.". . .

WHITE ATROCITIES

How do the whites act when they recapture the *San Dominick*? Do their civilized natures emerge? Are their acts marked by Christian, civilized justice? The deposition provides some answers. In it we find evidence of white barbarity balancing that of the slaves. Several Negroes were killed at night while shackled to the ring bolts on deck. Martinez Gola was caught aiming a razor at the throat of a chained slave. Bartholomew Barlo was stopped from stabbing a shackled black. Perhaps the most damning illustration of white barbarity is the account of Babo's punishment: "dragged to the gibbet at the tail of a mule, the black met his voiceless end. The body was burned to ashes; but for many days the head, that hive of subtlety, fixed on a pole in the Plaza, met, unabashed, the gaze of the whites.". . . The description of Babo's execution [is] an indictment of a society which, even within the framework of law, is as capable of barbarity as is the "unenlightened" savage. . . . By reserving Babo's death for the final paragraph and thereby emphasizing it, Melville reinforces what, throughout his fiction, he repeatedly stated—that no great disparity exists between the nonwhite savage and the white civilized man. The severed black head facing St. Bartholomew's church—an ironic and tragic juxtaposition of two worlds, two cultures, two races—renders incredible the argument that Melville has "whitened the whites." Following the above passage from *Typee*, Melville indicted "the white as the most ferocious animal on the face of the earth." In *Benito Cereno*, he shows both white and black as equally capable of ferocity, equally capable of reducing men to the level of brutes. Babo, it should be noted, was a slave in both black and white societies. In merging the "civilized" brutality of the whites with the animal ferocity of the blacks, Melville has dramatized the universality of the savage impulse. . . .

Babo deserves considerable credit for being the awesomely clever mastermind of a plot so well implemented that it almost succeeds. . . .

The mind that devised such a scheme may be a "hive of subtlety," but it is a mind which commands respect. Central to that scheme is Babo's masquerade as a menial. Like the mask of the confidence man, it is based on a shrewd understanding of the white man's attitudes toward the black. Babo is also to be respected for his determination and spirit. Never panicking, never faltering, even during the fury of the revolt, he steadfastly keeps in mind the main objective. Neither does he bow; captured, "he uttered no sound, and could not be forced to." And like the unquailing, kingly Atufal before the sickly Cereno, Babo even in death remains defiant, his head meeting "unabashed, the gaze of the whites." Depending on the degree to which one can sympathize with Babo's motives, the black's performance could be called heroic. One thing is certain: Babo is no inferior. His dominant traits are intelligence, determination, firmness of will and command, and defiant pride. Except in the beclouded mind of Delano, the stereotype darky complete with castanets and good-natured grin is not aboard the *San Dominick*; an individual is. We may admire or despise Babo, but our response is not dictated by his color; Melville has created a memorable human being. . . .

HUMAN SAVAGENESS

Benito Cereno is neither an abolitionist tract nor a condemnation of the Negro race. Evil and ferocity are not confined to the blacks; heroism and virtue are not the exclusive traits of the whites. Both blacks and whites are part of the humanity whose dark side Melville will not deny. Like the satyr on the stern-piece, Babo is part man, part beast. Like

Bembo of *Omoo*, he is man (in that his response to humiliation is courageously human) and devil (in that his vengeance takes a particularly vicious turn). But the white man, who ironically espouses a religion of charity, forgiveness, and brotherhood, is also a beast. Who can say where the blame rests for the carnage unleashed aboard the floating coffin? The untamed and demoniac forces rampant on the *San Dominick* characterize not a particular race, but all of mankind. *Benito Cereno* poses the problem with which Herman Melville grappled from *Typee* to *Billy Budd*: the "primeval savageness which ever slumbers in human kind, civilized or uncivilized."...

BARRIERS TO EQUALITY

In Melville's fiction the several races of mankind are inseparably intertwined, united by his acknowledgment of the individual's special worth. Through the interaction of characters of all colors, Melville dramatizes how in the ideal society the nonwhite should be regarded. The foolish, the cruel, the ignorant, and the sheltered categorize the nonwhite in accord with the role the "bland hypocrisies" of society assign him, that of inferior buffoon or of scowling savage; the humane and the wise see him as an individual to be liked or disliked for his human traits.... In [Melville's] fictional world, men have a fundamental claim to humanity. Such democratic faith is echoed and reechoed from the first book to the last. We see that faith in Tommo's warm admiration of the physical perfection and the harmonious social order of the "savage" Polynesians; in his indictment of the white race, which, in imposing its values on the Polynesians, is responsible for corroding the racial identity of these people; in the anger and pity evoked by the plight of Negro slaves in *Mardi*; in Redburn's recognition of the black man's humanity; in White-Jacket's acknowledgment of man, white or dark, as the image of God; in the "champions from the kingly commons," dark as well as white, embraced by Ishmael's "just spirit of equality"; in the striking resemblances between General Glendinning, John Paul Jones and Ethan Allen, and the Typee warriors and Queequeg; in the universe of *The Confidence-Man* and *Benito Cereno*, where black is indistinguishable from white; and, finally, in the simple recognition that the "handsome sailor"—a cynosure of "strength and beauty"—can be either a Billy Budd or a

Negro on a Liverpool dock.

The barrier to equality, Melville suggests, is the absence of mutual respect which, in turn, becomes mutual distrust. Significantly, the white man is usually the architect of the wall which separates the races. If Melville's nonwhites are scowling barbarians or grinning stereotypes, they are made so by the whites who refuse to acknowledge their humanity. The denial takes many forms: "wanton acts of cruelty" for "mere amusement" by white seamen who "hardly consider [Polynesians] human"; the humiliation and endless rounds of practical jokes inflicted on black seacooks; the brute level to which Negro slaves are degraded by the lash; the stares and grimaces of local greenhorns at the Queequegs, Samoas, and Lavenders; a Spaniard's racial insult flung at Daggoo; Stubb's abandoning "insignificant" Pip and ridiculing Fleece; river-boat passengers tossing pennies at the mouth of a crippled Negro; an American captain's fondness for Negroes as though they were Newfoundland dogs.

Such treatment is best explained by White-Jacket: ". . . There is something in us, somehow, that in the most degraded condition, we snatch at a chance to deceive ourselves into a fancied superiority to others, whom we suppose lower in the scale than ourselves." Melville's fictional world refutes this self-deception, this "fancied superiority" which degrades others. There can be no preeminent race, no mastery of one people over another in a world where white American heroes are remarkably similar to dusky Polynesians; where "the New Zealander's tattooing is not a prodigy nor the Chinaman's way an enigma"; where "we may have civilized bodies and yet barbarous souls"; where "primeval savageness ever slumbers in human kind, civilized or uncivilized"; where "a man can be honest in any sort of skin"; where Indians, Orientals, Polynesians, Negroes, and Caucasians are "sprung from one head, and made in one image." Such a world, dark as well as bright, is Herman Melville's "common continent of men."

Melville's *Battle-Pieces* Is Moving Civil War Poetry

Stanton Garner

In the following article, Stanton Garner analyzes several of Melville's poems from his Civil War collection, *Battle-Pieces*. Garner takes issue with critics who argue that Melville was trying to "cash in on" the Civil War, contending that the poems prove Melville's talent as a poet. In addition, Garner maintains that Melville, like a modern-day prophet, was trying to guide the nation away from making the same mistakes again. Stanton Garner's book, *The Civil War World of Herman Melville*, from which this viewpoint is taken, is both a biography and a work of literary criticism.

As the fighting died away, Herman began sustained work on *Battle-Pieces*. . . . Like the violent upheavals of the [Civil War] themselves, the immediate reactions of an artist to events were subject to excesses of grief, anxiety, anger, and exultation; it was necessary to wait until the flux of the conflict had subsided into a coherent memory. The end of the war, then, was the point at which Herman began to make his book. . . .

It deals with a war so lavish in emotion and so profligate in event that to the present day it affords historians an inexhaustible field for inquiry. . . .

"THE APPARITION"

"The Apparition (A Retrospect)" was inspired by Frank Bartlett's experience in the great mine explosion at Petersburg. Herman could imagine the horror of the Confederate soldiers as they felt the solidity of the earth swell and burst beneath their feet, which suggested an important qualification of the meliorative tone of the latter part of *Battle-Pieces*. The poem is central to the meaning of the book in that it focuses and completes the initiation into war's horrors of earlier poems. It is final proof that the worldview of the "bachelor," who sees only the cheerful, comfortable side of the human condition, is incomplete and therefore false. That had been the error of those who had trusted in Raphael and Michael. This poem invokes a pastoral, Shenandoah-like America, a green and growing world signified here in Herman's poetic shorthand as "Solidity." Even after John Brown's shadow had fallen across the "pastoral green," the nation remained confident in its promise and its belief in an orgiastic future. But Solidity is not the way of the world, in the past or in the future. It is only an appearance concealing behind it a central fact of man's existence, Satan's "eruptions of a darkness always lurkingly present in human affairs." When the union is severed and the consequences are felt, America is blasted by an eruption of violence and malignity. In a convulsion, a "goblin-mountain" pushes up from beneath the verdure and fertility is replaced by marl, slag, and clinkers: "The unreserve of Ill was there," Satanic ill. Yet before the senses can fully absorb and the mind comprehend, the eruption disappears as though it had never existed, leaving behind it the great philosophical lesson of the war: "Solidity's a crust— / The core of fire below." The appearance of wholeness returns, but the existence of Satan has been established for all time; he retreats back to his abyss to await another moment when man's imperfection will renew his opportunity to seize the reins of events. Preserving the memory of the goblin-mountain is a major purpose of *Battle-Pieces*: if future fields for fight are congealing beneath the sea, awareness must protect the nation from again becoming the battleground. An entire people must be educated to distrust the illusion that Solidity is dependable and to prevent the apparition from appearing again. . . .

"AMERICA"

"America" is more notable for its vision than it is for its originality. Embodying America in a conventional feminine figure, it is an allegory that the general public would have understood, and as such it has been criticized as tepid and derivative and as a "ritual of a sleazy sort." But when it is understood as a culminating point of *Battle-Pieces*, a counterpoint to "The Apparition," and the final appearance of the mother figure introduced in "Apathy and Enthusiasm," it gains purpose and dignity. To quote Milder, the poem "shapes the confusion of events [of the preceding poems] into an over-arching national myth and clarifies the process of moral growth the poems have occasioned in the reader all along."

SHILOH: A REQUIEM

In a poem from Battle-Pieces *entitled "Shiloh," Melville speaks of the aftermath of that battle.*

> Skimming lightly, wheeling still,
>   The swallows fly low
> Over the field in clouded days,
>   The forest-field of Shiloh—
> Over the field where April rain
> Solaced the parched ones stretched in pain
> Through the pause of night
> That followed the Sunday fight
>   Around the church of Shiloh—
> The church so lone, the log-built one,
> That echoed to many a parting groan
>   And natural prayer
>   Of dying foemen mingled there—
> Foemen at morn, but friends at eve—
>   Fame or country least their care:
> (What like a bullet can undeceive!)
>   But now they lie low,
> While over them the swallows skim,
>   And all is hushed at Shiloh.

If "The Apparition" invokes the dark side of the war experience, this poem is a reminder that there is also hope. It begins with a vision of an American flag "where the wings of a sunny Dome expand"—suggesting the Capitol dome as well as the firmamental dome—with the antebellum land reposing "in peace below." In this green world, the children (the states and the citizens alike) of the young mother were "folded to the exulting heart / Of young Maternity." Then in the earlier days of the war the flag streamed not in peace but "in fight / When tempest mingled with the fray," and over the flagstaff there was "ambiguous lightning." As her children strove "Valor with Valor" in their fierce Pride and Despair, "the lorn Mother speechless stood, / Pale at the fury of her brood." The children descend into Satan's primal world while the mother lapses into unconsciousness, seemingly dead and wrapped as on a bier in the flag that had once flown so grandly above. It is the dark night of the soul for America, as in sleep she sees the dark truths that *Battle-Pieces* has revealed. Her face is contorted by the vision "revealing earth's foundation bare, / And Gorgon in her hidden place." It is fearful to see "so foul a dream upon so fair a face." In short, she has glimpsed the "unreserve of Ill" of "The Apparition," the "core of fire" beneath Solidity. The "foul" dream serves the additional purpose of affirming that "the world's fairest hope linked with man's foulest crime" in "Misgivings" refers not to slavery but to the fratricidal battle which threatened "the Founders' dream."

The nightmare is necessary as a prelude to spiritual renewal. Thus America awakens with slavery crushed ("At her feet a shivered yoke") and with "no trace of passion or of strife" in her "clear calm look." The hope for the future lies in the belief that the nation may not only survive the primitive passions of war but may also transcend them into greatness. America is no longer innocent; pain has purified her and knowledge has repressed her triumph; her power is dedicated and her hope informed. "Law on her brow and empire in her eyes. / So she, with graver air and lifted flag" stands on her promontory, the shadow that had fallen over her gone. The innocent and ineffective Raphael has been replaced on the pinnacle by the newly wise and mature America who, ideally, will never again fall victim to Satan. Thus the outcome of the war would justify its terrible suffering.

It is disquieting to read of an America with "empire in her eyes," since that suggests a nation vying with the crowns of Europe for colonial dominion in Africa, Asia, and the Pacific isles. Indeed, it would hardly be surprising, considering his late brother Gansevoort's oratory on behalf of the annexation of Texas, to learn that Herman's vision of America included Manifest Destiny in the sense of southwestern territorial expansion that would stretch the nation's borders from Atlantic to Pacific; *that* empire was already all but achieved, its borders essentially established. But he would not have approved of interference with primitive cultures, as on the island paradises of the Pacific, the spoliation of which by "Paul Pry" with his "Pelf and Trade" he lamented in his late poem, "To Ned." Empire in this poem may be understood in terms of Frederick Merk's "Mission," as distinguished from territorial aggrandizement: the capture of men's minds rather than their lands. The Mission of America is "to redeem the Old World by high example": the example of liberty, democracy, human rights, public spiritedness, compassion, and all of the other ideals that the nation, however imperfectly, stood for.... The American empire would come to pass when, from one margin of the globe to the other, feudalism had given way to democratic equality....

SLAVERY

For the most part, Herman avoided the issue of slavery. He might not have written any poem at all on the subject had he not attended the National Academy of Design Exhibition. ...Hundreds of paintings were hung in the North, South, East, and West Rooms and in a central corridor. It was in the corridor that Herman saw Sanford Gifford's "The Coming Storm," which inspired his poem about Edwin Booth. War illustrators, such as Thomas Nast and Winslow Homer, were represented by camp scenes, while other artists exhibited a large cross section of the most memorable works of a notable era in American art: Albert Bierstadt, Frederick Church, Eastman Johnson, William Sidney Mount, Asher B. Durand, William Bradford, George Innes, William M. Hunt, Jasper Cropsey, Thomas Hicks, and Elihu Vedder, among others.

The paintings by Vedder, which included "The Arab Slave," "Jane Jackson, Formerly a Slave," "Lonely Spring," and "A Lost Mind," hung in the West Room. The *New York Times* critic was both impressed and perplexed by them. He admired their "absolute power," but he was put off by their darkness and by their enigmatic character. About the portrait of Jane Jackson, he decided that "the subject is not a very attractive one, but it is handled with great fidelity and strength." For Herman, the subject *was* attractive, and Vedder's dark vision was preferable to the conventionality of much of the show.

The inspiration for Herman's "'Formerly a Slave': An idealized Portrait, by E. Vedder, in the Spring Exhibition of the National Academy, 1865," then, was a rendering by a painter to whom he was particularly attracted of an old black peanut-seller encountered by Vedder on the streets of New York. Although "the sufferance of her race" is plain in her face, for her "too late deliverance dawns." Like the old crippled slave of "The Scout toward Aldie," she has no youth to squander on dreams, on education, and on personal fulfillment. For many like her, and even much younger, a past of servitude has bred a present of ignorance, dependence, and long-ingrained servility that makes them unemancipated slaves of fate. Even her son (a Union soldier, she told Vedder) may never gain full freedom. But "her children's children they shall know / The good withheld from her" as they break free of the yoke of the American black's special inheritance, and then emancipation will have come to an entire people. Thus from "down the depth of thousand years" she sees the good that is to come—not to her but to hers—and "her dusky face is lit with sober light.". . .

THE FINAL POEM

The final poem of *Battle-Pieces,* "A Meditation: Attributed to a Northerner after attending the last of two funerals from the same homestead—those of a National and a Confederate Officer (brothers), his kinsmen, who had died from the effects of wounds received in the closing battles," is set in a separate section following "Lee in the Capitol," thereby suggesting, along with its content and tone, that it is another late addition. Its heavily contrived dramatic situation refers back to the brothers who had parted in hatred in "Apathy and Enthusiasm," but where another poet might have focused his attention on the sentimental cliché of the fraternal deaths, Herman chose instead to dwell on the brotherly bonds that the war never sundered.

It is largely a compendium of recorded incidents of the war, and there were many, in which the bond of common humanity reasserted itself. An emissary from one army finds old friends in the other with whom to spend a warm social hour. Soldiers fronting each other at close range exchange compliments and food instead of bullets. In an event that occurred before Marye's Heights at Fredericksburg, a Confederate soldier risks his life to bring water to a Union soldier lying gravely wounded between the battling armies. Generals who had been schoolmates at West Point battle one another, and when armies pause during a truce, friends and relatives glimpse each other across the chasm of divided loyalties: "And something of a strange remorse / Rebelled against the sanctioned sin of blood, / And Christian wars of natural brotherhood." At such moments they feel "the god within the breast" and doubt "each plea and subterfuge of earth," asking rebelliously, "Can Africa pay back this blood / Spilt on Potomac's shore?"

In 1866, while the nation was searching for the means of reunification, this godly pull of brotherhood had special significance. If the two sides were to become one again, it would be necessary to abandon the vindictiveness of Emerson and Stevens: "*'The South's the sinner!'* Well, so let it be; / But shall the North sin worse, and stand the Pharisee?" To feel the old bonds now is as manly—and at least as easy—as it was to feel them during the bloodiest moments of the war. Southerners inspired admiration for their bravery in battle; so much the more should they be treated with dignity now: "When Vicksburg fell, and the moody files marched out, / Silent the victors stood, scorning to raise a shout." If Herman had refused to celebrate the starvation of the Vicksburg defenders in his battle poems, now he could find in their surrender a trenchant example of respect for the defeated to guide the North. . . .

THE BRADY OF CIVIL WAR VERSE

Like *Moby-Dick, Clarel,* and *Billy Budd, Battle-Pieces* is the only book of its type ever written or ever likely to be written in America. Calling him "the Brady [Matthew, Civil War photographer] of Civil War verse," [critic Newton] Arvin claims that "Melville is the first poet in English to realize the meaning of modern technological warfare." But the book is more. In the realm of imaginative literature, it is the only important attempt ever made to grapple intellectually with a distinctly *American* war, which is not to deny that there are other notable war books with different aims. There have been only two *American* wars, wars in which Americans battled to create and define their political identity, the Revolutionary War and the Civil War. All others have been foreign expeditions. But these two were truly national, the first the crucible from which the new country was poured and the second the agony that seems to have been necessary to resolve unanswered questions about the national identity. Of the Revolutionary War, it is safe to say that it inspired no literary work of distinction other than prose advocacy. Those who experienced it left that task to future writers. . . . But these later works have never attained the first rank of literary merit. . . .

A POLITICAL BOOK

Battle-Pieces is entire unto itself. It is a political book. . . . Fogle has described Melville's "public role" as "an unofficial poet laureate of the American nation, who tries to register in poetry the impact and the scope of the Civil War in all representative aspects." Melville asked what nation this was, why Fate had dashed it against the rocks of war, and what sort of future might await it. That future could be bright if the author were permitted to enter the "historical breach" caused by the war "to help refound America upon a worthier ideal of character." The resulting poetry is the product of restless wisdom, sharp sight and insight, high patriotism, unfailing compassion, religious fatalism, both tragic and epic intentions, and the poetic will to weave these elements into a single, unified expression. It is a revolt against the genteel and ideal sentiment that told readers what they wished to hear about the nobility and sanctity of their cause and their warriors, substituting grittiness that told readers who they were, what they had done and why, in what direction they might be headed, and what hope remained that the American experiment might yet ennoble mankind. It is a literary achievement that could have come only from Herman Melville. . . .

THE WAR AND MELVILLE'S BELIEFS

It is doubtful that the war revolutionized Melville's religious beliefs, but it affected them by subjecting them to the severest of tests. If one believed in a god at all, one was forced to reconcile the ravages and sufferings of war, and even the outbreak of the war itself, to that belief. What kind of god would decree such suffering? . . .

In *Battle-Pieces*, the analogues to Ormuzd, the son, and Ahriman, his evil twin, the subordinate gods of constructive good and anarch evil in Zoroastrianism, are, to further confuse matters, named Christ and Satan. In a book of war poems, there is little room for Christ except as "the Forgiver" of "The Swamp Angel," whose wish it is to convert those who would celebrate the sufferings of the innocent. He appears most frequently in the "Supplement," where both charity and benevolence are Christian principles. The war is the province of Satan, its instigator. He is the god of dissonance, malignancy, disruption, derangement, and suffering. He is the author of original sin, of which war is the ultimate celebration. In "Misgivings," he is the spirit of Nature's "dark side." Yet he cannot prevent even war from having a favorable outcome—because in the end God's plan governs.

It is difficult to determine precisely what Melville meant

Christ and Satan to be. It is possible that they are intended to be genuine deities—or angels—but it is equally possible that they represent elements, good and evil, of man's moral or psychological nature. In the latter case, Christ would represent man's higher values, his compassion, forgiveness, conscience, while Satan would represent his innate malevolence, belligerence, hatreds, bigotries, callousness. Nevertheless, in *Billy Budd* Melville implicitly deplored the decline of "that lexicon which is based on Holy Writ" and protested against the idea that a theological explanation of evil would be "subject to the charge of being tinctured with the biblical element." Other members of Melville's celestial host are canards. Raphael and Michael are human fabrications, and the holy angels who stand behind the Union sailors at Mobile Bay are no more than baroque figurines introduced for ornament. Thus the population of Melville's unseen world numbers three, at most.

It is safe to say that, other than Father Mapple, Melville never created a clergyman that he liked, and at the time of *Battle-Pieces* this anticlericism was in full flower. If the battle-poems offered him little opportunity to introduce clerics as dramatic characters, in "The Battle of Stone River" he did so by allusion, recalling that during the Wars of the Roses "monks blessed the fratricidal lance, / And sisters scarfs could twine." He would take up that theme again in *Billy Budd*, in which the chaplain, a man of Christ who should oppose war, permits himself to be enlisted in the ranks of Satan's warriors. He is the "church" in "church and state," an instrument of feudal tyranny. In "The Scout toward Aldie," the chaplain, far from sustaining others spiritually, is intent on curing his own spiritual ailments. Melville's complaint was not that these clergymen were evil or ill-intentioned men, only that they were inadequate to the daunting task they undertook. . . .

AN END TO HOPE

There was only one antidote to the pain and suffering, the prospect that fear and pity would guide the nation toward a better future in which it would abandon the follies and vanities of the past to embrace faith, humility, Christian charity, and its destiny of leading the world toward a future of moral progress. At some midwar point, Melville dedicated his artistry to that future, and when the government divided and faltered over the proper postwar path, he was ready with his pen to lead the way toward justice and tolerance. He was wrong in believing that he would be heard, but that miscalculation does not invalidate the achievement of *Battle-Pieces*.

Thus for five intense years Melville was a man dedicated to a cause, not the man of uncertainty and clouded aims he had been before the war. His subsequent fall was as precipitous as his ascent had been steep. A new America was emerging, but it was not his chastened mother. His hopes for national rededication were shattered and his poetic aspirations were crushed. Never again would he delude himself into thinking that he might be recognized in his own time, nor would he ever again see himself as the bard of national destiny.

Israel Potter as a Historical Novel

Alfred Kazin

Alfred Kazin is a well-known literary critic and writer praised for his works *On Native Grounds* and the autobiographical *New York Jew*. In the following article, Kazin argues that although Israel Potter is a rather inept and uninteresting hero, Melville prevents the novel from being mundane by using it as a foil to characterize several well-known historical figures.

Israel Potter: His Fifty Years of Exile has probably been the least read of Melville's novels up to now; it has rarely been available outside of Melville's collected works. The book has a curious history, and it is certainly a curious book. Though Melville's heroes are mostly himself under various disguises (he was complicated enough to be both Ishmael and Ahab), nowhere did he describe his psychic monomania of exile, drift, homelessness, so pointedly as he did in emphasizing Israel Potter's continual misfortunes and final beggary for almost fifty years. Yet never did he have a character less reflective, less like himself, than Israel Potter. What Israel shares with Herman Melville is "exile" seemingly perpetual, exile as a lifetime experience, exile as a feeling about life unexplained by the circumstances of exile. Fortunately, it is not Israel who dominates the book but Israel's often cliffhanger adventures. And the book has some historical actors—Benjamin Franklin, John Paul Jones, Ethan Allen—who are as powerful in their way as Melville was in his secret soul, powerful as only a great writer can be.

In 1854 Melville picked up a ragged, slatternly paperback book called *Life and Remarkable Adventures of Israel R. Potter, A Native of Cranston, R.I.* This was the hack "life and adventures" of a Revolutionary War veteran, an agile but by no means unusual man who had been captured by the British at Bunker Hill, was taken to England as a prisoner in January, 1776, escaped, was recaptured, but served under John Paul Jones in the famous battle of the *Bon Homme Richard* with the *Serapis.* Israel Potter was an unlucky fellow; even after the victory of the American cause, he was unable to get home to Rhode Island until 1823. He lived out much of his English "exile" among the poorest of the poor in London, weaving cane chairs and crying his wares.

The *Life and Remarkable Adventures of Israel R. Potter* is a conventionally written, stilted autobiography of a bizarre life that became so by accident. Israel was, you might say, one of history's sad sacks, and his book is not stimulating. Melville, back in 1849, visiting London, wrote in his diary that he "looked over a lot of ancient maps of London. Bought one (A.D. 1776) for 3 & 6 pence. I want to use it in case I serve up the Revolutionary narrative of the beggar." In short, when Melville was still the well-known and "successful" author of such best sellers as *Typee* and *Omoo,* and before he had injured his reputation (!) by baffling his audience with the "metaphysical nonsense" of *Moby Dick,* Melville was thinking of exploiting, for his own novelistic purposes the undistinguished, pathetic figure of Israel R. Potter. Melville had some vague plans in the back of his head—it was possible that he might yet "serve up the Revolutionary narrative of the beggar."

MELVILLE'S FASCINATION WITH ISRAEL POTTER

Something about the extraordinary adventures but miserably rootless life of Israel R. Potter fascinated Melville. The "Revolutionary" period was one of heroic individuals, like Melville's own grandfathers. But even more, the idea of using another man's actual and reported life appealed to Melville's habitual strategy as an author. This strategy was always to convert some piece of actual experience, so long as it was bizarre, exotic, unduplicated by the middle-class respectable life Melville was leading as an author, husband and father into a loose, episodic, nicely spiced novel of adventure for the general public. But this genial popular adventure story also had to dramatize Melville's favorite idea of himself as a literary warrior at odds with his time. A book had to dramatize the epic struggle with the universe of Melville's own rebellious idiosyncrasy. This explains the ups and downs of his literary fortunes.

Melville, born into the best society of New York (Dutch and British), a descendant on both sides of famous (and dashing) Revolutionary War generals, had been driven, like his alter ego, Ishmael, into the "wilderness." His father, a hard-driven New York merchant, had gone bankrupt, then gone to pieces and died when his son was thirteen. Melville went to sea as a cabin boy; at twenty-two he embarked in a whaler from New Bedford on the three-and-a-half-year voyage that was to lead him to the South Seas, and into every possible scrape and adventure as a sailor. This was his making as an author. Melville began his literary career with best-selling nonfiction novels, *Typee* and *Omoo*, based on his adventures in the South Seas. Then, with *Mardi*, Melville showed that he could write a bad "visionary" novel to please himself—then turn back to more acceptable books, like *Redburn* and *White-Jacket*, just to keep the pot boiling. He could also, as all the world knows now but didn't during his lifetime, write a book of headlong genius, *Moby Dick*, that would for all practical purposes sink him as a professional author.

By 1855, when Melville finally did "serve up the Revolutionary narrative of the beggar," Melville was thirty-six, had published seven books, had a wife and children, but was no longer considered a reliable literary property by publishers in New York and London. He wrote as fast as any Irving Wallace or Harold Robbins who nowadays serves up a "quick read" for the hurried man dashing to a plane. But though Melville's works usually dealt with out-of-the-way adventures in remote parts of the world, this strange philosophical streak in him, this determination to be perpetually in mutiny against a genteel American upper-crust that claimed to have the final answers to all human questions and difficulties, had made Herman Melville a most difficult and unassimilable literary property.

ISRAEL POTTER AS AUTOBIOGRAPHY

Here is the personal drama behind *Israel Potter*—this peculiar, fascinating, uneven, often richly comic book. We cannot overlook the (still?) surprising fact that a leading American author (admittedly of somewhat dubious reputation) took a hack book and turned it into an allegory of his own life. Melville wrote it just to make some money. But with his unstoppable creative force he turned *Israel Potter* into a satiric picaresque novel that is much more about the real Herman Melville than it is about the real Israel Potter.

Yet there *was* a real Israel Potter. And in this book he remains an historic personage even though Melville moves his birthplace from Rhode Island to the Berkshires, then puts him through adventures that are not in the original text or are jauntily expanded out of all resemblance to the humdrum original.

Most strikingly, Melville puts into his "Revolutionary narrative" one of the great satires on Benjamin Franklin, plus a brilliantly overcolored view of Ethan "Ticonderoga" Allen as an American Samson among the (British) Philistines who have captured him. There is a view of the American Navy's John Paul Jones as a restless masculine desperado who feels cooped up to the point of madness when he is not fighting. In two successive chapters, Melville gives us a marvelously old-fashioned naval battle—John Paul Jones's almost suicidal victory in the *Bon Homme Richard* over the *Serapis*—a gory killing fight to the finish that went on into the night under the light of the moon over the Cliffs of Dover, from which a crowd of spectators gaped.

Melville's *Israel Potter* is at its best as a book about American men in the old, slashing, heroic style of romantic war, escapade, incessant movement. It is a book about warriors who have the character of brigands and pirates, ferocious toughies who fight for the pleasure of fighting, and who are never so happy as when they are knocking down the enemy with everything in sight. At Bunker Hill, writes Melville, "Not one American musket in twenty had a bayonet to it. So, wielding the stock right and left, the terrible farmers, with hats and coats off, fought their way among the furred grenadiers, knocking them right and left, as seal-hunters on the beach knock down with their clubs the Shetland seal."

BENJAMIN FRANKLIN

Israel Potter is about men who are ruled less by loyalty to a specific place or country than by their own irresistible feeling for adventure, risk, deception. The portrait of Benjamin Franklin is a masterpiece of irreverence. Franklin was without doubt a genius, as he was certainly one of the most useful men who ever trod the American earth. But also an intriguer, entrepreneur, publicist, speculator, and above all a wily old hypocrite, Franklin is beautifully portrayed by Melville as a man of infinite cunning, as classical in his wiles and stratagems as Ulysses or the Biblical Jacob.

The scenes between Israel and Benjamin Franklin are straight comedy—with poor, innocent, always besought and unlucky Israel as the straight man. Franklin is shown as the gay deceiver and unctuous man of affairs in all things— above all, the canniest man with a penny in American history before Calvin Coolidge. "Every time he comes in," poor Israel soliloquizes dolefully, "he robs me; with an air all the time, too, as if he were making me presents."

John Paul Jones, who cries out when he is not on duty— "My God, why was I not born a Czar!"—is deliciously a savage. "He was a rather small, elastic, swarthy man, with an aspect of a disinherited Indian Chief in European clothes. An unvanquishable enthusiasm intensified to perfect sobriety, couched in his savage, self-possessed eye." He runs his warships right into one English harbor after another. And spiking the cannon in Whitehaven, talks to them like a Shakespearean brigand—"I'll tongue-tie the thunderers."

This emphasis on heroic, military, hell-for-leather grappling with the enemy is the really decisive element in Melville's narrative. It reflects Melville's own passionate admiration for masculine power, headlong independence at any price, a damn-the-torpedoes resistance to the hindrances that life may raise. John Paul Jones is also plainly mad; the American "Samson" in English captivity, Ethan Allen, is willfully mad, histrionically defiant, a ham acting it up. Franklin is wily to the point of being inhuman. But these are men, as we say now, in the "classic" mold—they are meant to portray the American Revolution as perhaps the last time when men could be heroes (and cutthroats) on an unlimited scale. Melville is amused by his characters, but he loves them and he loves a time when the heroic individual like Franklin, Jones, Allen, seemed to incarnate fierce strength and unquestioning self-trust. In a revolutionary period such men incarnated the energy, the new hope, of revolution.

Melville felt that to be a man of power, a true hero and rebel in behalf of "nature," you had to be somewhat touched. Like Herman Melville. Nature, the "world," are not "sane," only society tries to be. The heroic individual, striking out for a vision that exists nowhere but in his own head, does so at the expense of his "balance."

About John Paul Jones, Melville says, typically,

> The career of this stubborn adventurer signally illustrates the idea that since all human affairs are subject to organic disorder, since they are created in and sustained by a sort of half-disciplined chaos, hence he who in great things seeks success must never want for smooth water, which never was and never will be, but with what straggling method he can, dash with all his derangements at his object, leaving the rest to Fortune.

Israel Potter is thus a very personal and positive novel about masculine force. The vitality is mock-heroic, lovingly satiric about American demigods like Franklin. But what of Israel Potter himself? Israel, as his Biblical name testified in Melville's time, is the perpetual victim and wanderer. He is the man things happen to—he is the dummy on whom Melville, pent up as usual in this strange, uneven book, put all the pain of his own wandering, his orphanage, his bereftness from God and society.

Poor Israel! He never really makes it. He is always out of luck. Although his creator, Herman Melville, does give him a yellow mane and once calls him a "lion," Israel is really the average man, caught up in a series of adventures and escapes. Melville was not at his best writing about the average man. But fortunately, it is not Israel himself who holds our attention in this book. It is Israel as the occasion for Melville to write about Bunker Hill, Israel as an occasion for Melville to write about Franklin, John Paul Jones, George III, various English radical sympathizers with the American Revolution, Paris during the American Revolution. Melville's versatile, comic, beautifully extreme talent came through in this book despite every possible handicap from Israel Potter himself.

Themes in *The Confidence-Man*

H. Bruce Franklin

H. Bruce Franklin was a professor of English and American literature at Rutgers University in New Jersey. A well-known critic, Franklin's several books include *Prison Literature in America, Robert A. Heinlein: America as Science Fiction,* and a work on Melville, *The Wake of the Gods.* In the following article, Franklin lays out what he believes are the primary themes in *The Confidence-Man.* Franklin contends that the book is both an adept social commentary and a complex mythological work.

America in the 1850's was a jungle in which all kinds of hunters pursued their quarry: slaves, factory workers, buffalo, Indians, Mexicans, Mormons, Catholics, Protestants, gold, land, and suckers. American troops had just seized almost half of Mexico, were now busy exterminating Indians from Florida to Oregon, and were preparing to attack the Mormons in Utah. Slavery had already caused much blood to flow, and the nation was on the brink of civil war. Bands of killers roamed almost at will on both sides of the Mississippi and far to the west, undaunted by meeting the heads of other killers stuck on poles. Violence came from the Gold Rush, land claims, competing settlements, economic catastrophes, obscure feuds, racism, and plain blood lusts. This is the immediate world of *The Confidence-Man,* which refers again and again to the violent events of this world and presents many kinds of men who had their being in these events.

But, though the scene is the central Mississippi, the symbolic center of America, the story contains the violence of many human places and times, from primitive tribes to the ancient Greek and Roman conquerors, from Phalaris and Nero to Torquemada, Cesare Borgia, and Pizarro, from the

From *The Confidence Man* by Herman Melville, edited, with an introduction and annotation, by H. Bruce Franklin. Copyright ©1967 by The Bobbs-Merrill Company, Inc. Reprinted by permission of the author and Prentice Hall, Upper Saddle River, New Jersey.

French Revolution to the revolutions of 1848–1849 and the Crimean War, which had just ended. Only one physical blow is struck on board the riverboat *Fidèle*, but its decks are slippery with the blood of history.

All the varieties of fraud and swindling are also here. On board the *Fidèle* are American representatives of herbdoctors, land agents, counterfeiters, impostors, charity agents, card sharps, divines, transcendental philosophers, con men of all kinds. They and their victims discuss, quote, and reenact the roles of the other con men of history, such as Plato, Pontius Pilate, Seneca, Augustine, Machiavelli, Bacon, Rochefoucauld, Chesterfield, and P.T. Barnum.

Many American types and American figures are passengers on the *Fidèle*. While we are on this ornate riverboat we are floating down the Mississippi River in the middle of nineteenth-century America, surrounded by local forms, local customs, local language, local characters. But just as black turns out to be an appearance of white, this West is also the East, and this time conjoins past with future.

FICTION, READERS, CHARACTERS, AUTHOR

The Confidence-Man makes many extraordinary demands on the reader. By reference, allusion, parody, and quotation, it appropriates and incorporates whole works into itself: many of Shakespeare's plays, many books of the Bible, Ovid's *Metamorphoses*, the *Aeneid*, *Paradise Lost*, and numerous other works are as integral to *The Confidence-Man* as the little stories told by its own characters. Furthermore, some of these characters are caricatures of historical personages (such as Diogenes, Cooper, Socrates, Emerson, Timon, Thoreau, Poe) and others represent mythic figures (such as Manco Capac, Christ, Orpheus, Satan, Vishnu, Buddha)....

Nothing in *The Confidence-Man* is wasted, misplaced, or merely decorative. The difficulties of syntax are not mere rhetorical flourishes or meaningless obscurities but constant invitations to the reader both to see all the multiple possibilities they create and to feel the sinuous rhythms and sinister weavings that are entrapping him in a dialectical web. Only a few of the ever present syntactical snares are annotated. Many, many of the words of *The Confidence-Man*, including its title, are significant puns.... Nothing in the book, from the most physical of objects to the most metaphysical of arguments, can, in the last analysis, be separated from every other thing in the book; so the cross-references in the footnotes only hint of the intricacy of the book's design.

Perhaps the most perplexing thing about the book is its diabolical suggestiveness. Elaborate solutions for all problems and mysteries are suggested; but they turn out to be incomplete or ambiguous. Hints are dropped about financial chicanery, religious imposture, physical disease, and sexual perversion; but they usually remain only hints. Darkness obscures all lights. The book ends by asserting that "something further *may* follow of this Masquerade." Behind and through all appearances peeps an author who suggests that he knows all. He asks the reader for his confidence while making it impossible to hear that word again without a most suggestively knowing smile.

FAITH IN MAN?

The Confidence-Man at first may seem to be a debate about the question, Should one have confidence in Man? One should resist the temptation to read the book as an argument for or against this position. One must also resist the temptation to read it as an unresolved debate; the debate serves to establish a dialectic, and the dialectic serves not to analyze the world that is but to create a new cosmos out of the materials of an old chaos. The principal materials of that old chaos exist within each reader, and it is he who is asked to re-form Man by entering a world in which an author and he define each other in terms of objects and characters they join in creating.

A reader begins, innocently perhaps, trying to read this book as though it were a novel. If he is a good novel-reader, he pays careful attention to the words and the physical objects and actions created out of these words. In the very first words of the book the reader discovers that the actions about to be described take place on April Fools' Day. At this point, he may suspect that the title character is going to be playing tricks on other characters; he may even suspect that the author is going to be playing tricks on him. But will he suspect the possibility that each physical object and action may be an All-Fools' joke because he will either see that it is not physical or else become its victim? Everything he is to see will be like a left-handed monkey wrench, a skyhook, or a can of striped paint, that is, a verbal thing, a tricky fiction created by the interaction of at least two minds. The first action of the book consists of a mysterious stranger coming upon a placard that presents "what purported to be a careful description" of "a mysterious impostor"; the stranger may read this description, but the reader may not. All he can read is the author's description of the stranger, who is a "lamblike" mute on a riverboat named the *Fidèle.*

Soon, however, the reader finds himself, together with the passengers on the *Fidèle,* receiving descriptions of all the subsequent avatars of the Confidence Man in the form of a list of "ge'mmen" reeled off by Black Guinea, a crippled Negro beggar, himself apparently a principal avatar. One by one these avatars appear in person, that is to say, in the author's words rather than in the words of Black Guinea, who is one of his characters. In this world a character creates his author by creating other characters who speak words formed by both of them.

CHARACTERS CREATE CHARACTERS

This only begins the involutions of fictive realities. Many subsequent characters at times become authors who create characters, some of whom then create other characters. Melville interpolates three chapters (14, 33, 44) addressed by the author to his readers about the relations among fiction, authors, characters, readers, and the rest of reality. Two characters try to get each other dizzy and confused with bad wine, cheap cigars, and a discussion of what authors mean by the words they put in the mouths of characters (Chapter 30). One of these characters later victimizes the other by telling him a story which he claims to have "told with the purpose of every storyteller—to amuse"; "Hence, if it seem strange to you, that strangeness is the romance; it is what contrasts it with real life; it is the invention, in brief, the fiction as opposed to the fact" (Chapter 35). One character hears a "true" story from two other characters who are evidently the same character in two different forms, and then repeats it, in a somewhat different version, to someone evidently a third form of the same character; we are not permitted to hear any of these versions because, as the authorial "we" tells us: "But as the good merchant could, perhaps, do better justice to the man than the story, we shall venture to tell it in other words than his, though not to any other effect" (Chapter 11). Now what in the world does it mean to do better justice to a man than to a story told about that man? And what then can "not to any other effect" possibly mean?

And what is all this hazy shadow play about? Part of the answer lies in the relations between man's imaginative reality, what he thinks, and man's identity, what he is.

Most of us wander through life identifying people in terms of such things as external characteristics (tall, fat, brown, bowlegged, eagle-beaked) or easily labeled groups (Negro, Methodist, Communist, worker, Indian) or more-or-less temporary states (rich, well-dressed, gloomy, angry, young, on a battlefield, in the cabin of the boat) and so forth. When we read most fictions, we are asked to behave in this usual way—only more so. If we are presented with a character described as a crippled Negro beggar on a Mississippi riverboat, we expect that character to remain the same except as he is changed by circumstances we are told about or may infer. He may get off the boat, stop begging, become healed, or, even more miraculously, lose his identity as a Negro; but he changes only as we accept the author's manipulations. If, in the next chapter, there appears a character who does not *appear* to be the same character, he *is* not the same character unless and until we are convinced that he is. Black Guinea's list exposes some of the consequences of these ordinary assumptions about fiction and other forms of existence.

BLACK GUINEA'S LIST

Black Guinea's list of the avatars of the Confidence Man is a list of only the most external characteristics:

> Oh yes, oh yes, dar is aboard here a werry nice, good ge'm-man wid a weed, and a ge'mman in a gray coat and white tie, what knows all about me; and a ge'mman wid a big book, too; and a yarb-doctor; and a ge'mman in a yaller west; and a ge'mman wid a brass plate; and a ge'mman in a wiolet robe; and a ge'mman as is a sodjer; and ever so many good, kind, honest ge'mmen more aboard what knows me and will speak for me, God bress 'em; yes, and what knows me as well as dis poor old darkie knows hisself, God bress him! Oh, find 'em, find 'em. . . .

We share the plight of the bystander who immediately wants to know, "But how are we to find all these people in this great crowd?" Apparently we are supposed to find out who people *are*—and who the Confidence Man *is*—by examining the colors each man wears, the objects he carries, and the role he plays. This is precisely what we see the people on the *Fidèle* doing and what we customarily do in our daily lives.

"Am I an Actor?"

*The Confidence-Man is a book full of characters who are all,
ostensibly, the same man—the confidence man. Throughout
the book, this man, in his various guises, casts aspersions on
the other characters' lack of faith, or "confidence" in their
fellow man. In this excerpt, "the man in gray," a guise for the
confidence man, accompanied by a reverend, accosts a one-
legged man about his conviction that a black crippled beggar,
Guinea, was really a white man masquerading as a black.*

"This reverend gentleman tells me, sir, that a certain
cripple, a poor negro, is by you considered an ingenious
impostor. Now, I am not unaware that there are some
persons in this world, who, unable to give better proof of
being wise, take a strange delight in showing what they
think they have sagaciously read in mankind by uncharita-
ble suspicions of them. I hope you are not one of these. In
short, would you tell me now, whether you were not merely
joking in the notion you threw out about the negro. . . .

"Well, he's just what I said he was."

"A white masquerading as a black?"

"Exactly."

The man in gray glanced at the young clergyman a
moment, then quietly whispered to him, "I thought you
represented your friend here as a very distrustful sort of
person, but he appears endued with a singular credulity.—
Tell me, sir, do you really think that a white could look the
negro so? For one, I should call it pretty good acting."

"Not much better than any other man acts."

"How? Does all the world act? Am *I*, for instance, an
actor? Is my reverend friend here, too, a performer?"

This is precisely what Black Guinea—almost certainly an
avatar of the Confidence Man—wants us to do, and what we
have to do in order to read the book with any coherence.

At the same time, Guinea's list, like everything else in *The
Confidence-Man*, contains its opposite. We do meet, in order,
characters explicitly described as a man with a weed, a man
in a gray coat and white tie, a man with a big book, and an
herb doctor, all of whom seem to be forms of the Confidence
Man. These are precisely half, the first half, of the particu-
larized characters in the list. Of the four who comprise the
second half, we meet only one described by the author as described by Guinea (this one is the second of the four). After

"Yes, don't you both perform acts? To do, is to act; so all doers are actors."

"You trifle.—I ask again, if a white, how could he look the negro so?"

"Never saw the negro-minstrels, I suppose?"

"Yes, but they are apt to overdo the ebony; exemplifying the old saying, not more just than charitable, that 'the devil is never so black as he is painted.' But his limbs, if not a cripple, how could he twist his limbs so?"

"How do other hypocritical beggars twist theirs? Easy enough to see how they are hoisted up."

"The sham is evident, then?"

"To the discerning eye," with a horrible screw of his gimlet one.

"Well, where is Guinea?" said the man in gray; "where is he?"...

"You forget," here said the young clergyman to the man in gray, "that yourself helped poor Guinea ashore."

"So I did, so I did; how unfortunate. But look now," to the other, "I think that without personal proof I can convince you of your mistake. For I put it to you, is it reasonable to suppose that a man with brains, sufficient to act such a part as you say, would take all that trouble, and run all that hazard, for the mere sake of those few paltry coppers, which, I hear, was all he got for his pains, if pains they were?"

"That puts the case irrefutably," said the young clergyman, with a challenging glance towards the one-legged man.

"You two green-horns! Money, you think, is the sole motive to pains and hazard, deception and deviltry, in this world. How much money did the devil make by gulling Eve?"

these eight particular characters, Guinea ends his list with "ever so many good, kind, honest ge'mmen," an indication that there are far more than ten (eight plus Guinea and the lamb-like man) shapes of the Confidence Man in this world and that all shapes may be ambiguous. Furthermore, Guinea speaks in a dialect, making any of his words possibly puns (as he hints by concluding "dis poor ole darkie is werry well *wordy* of all you kind ge'mmen's kind confidence").

Guinea's wordiness, like the muteness of the lamb-like man, expands until it fills the universe of *The Confidence-Man*; his list ultimately includes everybody. To perceive what is involved, one must read his list artfully, always following its movement through precision into ambiguity, through the particular to the universal—or apparently chaotic.

Number 1. "A werry nice, good ge'mman wid a weed." The first listed avatar seems the easiest to find. John Ringman appears with "a long weed on his hat" in Chapter 4 and then is referred to in the title of Chapter 5 as "The man with the weed." But to establish this identity we must assume that the author sticks to Guinea's terms, something later to be made dubious. We might, as one alternative, take Guinea's "weed" to mean tobacco, making each of the two confidence men who force cigars on the other in Chapter 30 a man with a weed; one of them, Frank Goodman, is certainly a "good man wid de weed," to use Guinea's very last words. Or we could take another common meaning of weed, "A covering; that which covers, spreads over vest or vestment, clothing or garment" (Richardson's *Dictionary*, 1844), and see the first of Guinea's listings to be as equivocal and far-reaching as the last. We may create this form of the Confidence Man wherever we see him.

Number 2. "A ge'mman in a gray coat and white tie." In Chapter 6 there appears "a man in a gray coat and white tie." But note that in Chapter 3, when a suspect Methodist minister attacks a cynical cripple, a voice cries out, "The white cravat against the world!"

Number 3. "A ge'mman wid a big book, too." In Chapter 9 there appears a man carrying a ledger-like transfer book; he is the president and transfer agent of the Black Rapids Coal Company. Several characters have small books, so we are asked to distinguish them from the Confidence Man by the size of their books. Then the last character mentioned in *The Confidence-Man* is discovered in possession of the big book of the gentlemen's cabin, the Bible. And both the reader and the author have a book, which may or may not be big.

Number 4. "A yarb-doctor." The relatively unambiguous first half of Guinea's list ends with one of the two unambiguous identifications; the only herb doctor appears just as the sun comes out from behind the clouds in Chapter 16.

Number 6. "A ge'mman wid a brass plate." The relatively unambiguous first half of the book ends with the other unambiguous identification; a man who wears a small brass plate around his neck, having just sold a hypothetical boy, gets ready to disembark as he passes a bluff called the Devil's Joke. As soon as he leaves, Chapter 23, the exact center of the book, describes the ambiguous twilight. After this, not one of Guinea's listings appears as Guinea had described.

Number 5. "A ge'mman in a yaller west" and Number 7. "A ge'mman in a wiolet robe." Neither of these two brightly colored forms is described by the author as described by Guinea. Either or both may be the sun, around which *The Confidence-Man*, like the world it images, revolves. The "man in cream-colors" who appears "at sunrise on a first of April" in the first sentence of the book might be viewed as a *gentle*man in a yellow vest ("vest," from the Latin *vestis*, meant any garment, particularly an outer garment, a robe or coat). Or the last character introduced in the book, a peddler-boy wearing a "fragment of an old linen coat, bedraggled and yellow," may be viewed as a *gamin* in a yellow vest. The herb doctor also wears a yellowish garment; several times he is pointedly identified as the man in the snuff-colored surtout. The sun, which comes out when he does, is then called "a golden huzzar." The Cosmopolitan calls all "moderns" "we golden boys," sees about Shakespeare a "hidden sun . . . at once enlightening and mystifying," and refers to the printing press as the sun, "god Apollo" who "dispenses the day."

As yellow is to the sunrise, violet is to the sunset. The two confidence men who confront each other in Chapters 25 through 35, the extraordinary Cosmopolitan and the ordinary riverboat con man, Charlie Noble, each wear something that resembles a violet robe. The Cosmopolitan "sported a *vest*ure barred with various hues, that of the cochineal predominating"; Charlie wears a "violet vest." A character who flits by in Chapter 6, a "gentleman in a ruby-colored velvet vest," would seem to be merely a red herring. But not to be dismissed is the intensely symbolic "robed man" on the ground-glass shade of the solar lamp in the final chapter; whether or not his robe is violet, the extinction of the solar lamp that illuminates him is much like the setting of the sun. And, after all, what makes colors?

Number 8. "A ge'mman as is a sodjer." Four of the *Fidèle*'s passengers play the role of playing the role of soldier. The lamb-like man, though "apparently a non-resistant," moves through the crowd "shield-like bearing his slate before him." Likewise, the Methodist minister, though he says he was thought "a non-combatant," is a "soldier-like," "martial-looking man . . . who in the Mexican War had been volunteer chaplain to a volunteer rifle-regiment." The man with the bandaged nose of Chapter 18, who walks "with a pace that seemed the lingering memento of the lock-step of convicts," is called a "poor wounded huzzar" by the herb doctor. The cripple of the following chapter, entitled "A Soldier of Fortune," claims to the herb doctor to have been crippled in prison but passes himself off to the other passengers as a wounded veteran of the Mexican War. He is both accused of belonging to "the Devil's regiment" (in *White-Jacket* Melville himself had said that any soldier "is but a fiend" who serves the Devil) and acclaimed as a fighter against "Fortune." He illustrates the art of "coming the old soldier," i.e., tricking like "a rogue who pretends to be an old soldier."

Besides these four passengers, there are other gentlemen who appear "as is a sodjer." There is the sun itself, likened to a "golden huzzar." There is a real soldier, Colonel John Moredock, one of the most important metaphysical (though not physical) passengers. The very word soldier—derived from *soldus* and literally meaning one who receives pay—suggests a fundamental ambiguity. And "sodjer" does not even necessarily mean "soldier." "Sodjer" (also spelled "sodger," "sojer," and "soger") in nautical usage meant, as Melville knew, "a red herring." Finally, all these possibilities combine in the possibilities foreshadowed by the final sentence of the book: "Something further may follow of this Masquerade." In apocalyptic visions of both the East and the West, the Savior in his last avatar will return as a destroying soldier.

THE CONFIDENCE-MAN AS MYTH

A reader familiar with no other myths than the Judeo-Christian ones may read through *The Confidence-Man* with a good partial understanding. He may see that the lamb-like man represents either Christ or Satan masquerading as Christ, that Guinea and the later avatars of the Confidence Man represent Satan, that the vision of the final chapter is filled with images from Revelation, and that the sequel hinted in the last sentence may be a fulfillment of that apocalypse. He may describe the Confidence Man's assumption of Christianity in familiar Western terms, such as diabolic, wicked, fiendish; and he may see this role as that of Satan or Anti-Christ.

However, this is not even half the mythic structure. One of

the great achievements of *The Confidence-Man* is its way of relating the principal Western myths to the principal Eastern myths and all myth to all other kinds of fiction. In *The Wake of the Gods: Melville's Mythology*, I discuss these relations in some detail; here I shall just summarize.

The Confidence-Man begins at sunrise on April 1st and ends shortly after midnight. All Fools' Day was generally assumed to be a remnant of the ancient great vernal festival, commemorating the rebirth of the sun, celebrated all around the Northern Hemisphere at the time of the vernal equinox, when the sun returns from "beneath" the equator. (The date of course shifts with the precession of the equinoxes.) Most authorities traced the rituals of All Fools' Day to the most ancient known vernal celebration, a Hindu masquerade called the Huli. These vernal rituals, held on the one day when the duration of light exactly equals and is about to exceed the duration of darkness (a division precisely reflected in the structure of *The Confidence-Man*), greeted the sun as the great savior-god returning from the realms of night, i.e., the Southern Hemisphere (whose best-known incarnation of the sun, Manco Capac, is likened to the lamb-like man in the first sentence of the book).

The Confidence Man is this sun, this god, this savior. But at the same time he is the darkness that obscures this sun (as Black Guinea when he holds up his "old coal-sifter of a tamborine" to indicate the sun, as the President of the Black Rapids Coal Company, as the Cosmopolitan when he extinguishes the last light in the book, a solar lamp); he is the god who struggles against this god; he is the destroyer. This identity of light and darkness, salvation and destruction, inherently alien to Christianity, lies at the heart of both Hinduism and Buddhism.

The avatars of the Confidence Man are quite literally *avatara*, that is, successive incarnations of the great Hindu god of salvation, Vishnu. The first major avatar of Vishnu is as a fish who recovers the lost sacred books; the first avatar of the Confidence Man is, among other things, an "Odd fish!" who brings to the world injunctions from the Bible. The second avatar is as a tortoise who upholds the world; the second avatar of the Confidence Man is as a "grotesque" figure who shuffles around on leather stumps, who lives "all 'long shore," and who holds his symbolic "coal-sifter of a tamborine" "high over his head." After this come eight other

major avatars and innumerable minor ones; Black Guinea
lists eight other major avatars and innumerable minor ones
("ever so many good, kind, honest ge'mmen"). For Hinduism
and for *The Confidence-Man* the two most important are the
last avatar which has come, Buddha, and the last avatar,
which is to come, Kalki.

The teachings of Buddha ("the enlightened"), who had
also the name of Gotamâ (*go*, senses, and *tamá*, darkness:
i.e., "he who brings darkness to the senses"), aimed toward
the achievement of *nirvana*, which means literally the ex-
tinguishing of a flame or lamp. According to Hindus (as opposed to Buddhists), Buddha was Vishnu incarnate as a deceiver, leading his enemies into spiritual darkness. The last
avatar of the Confidence Man is the Cosmopolitan, who finally extinguishes the last light, the solar lamp, and leads
man into the ensuing darkness.

In Hinduism, Vishnu the Preserver is one face of a three-
headed godhood, the Trimurti, whose other two faces are
Brahma the Creator and Siva the Destroyer. Brahma has no
role in the created world; but Siva, like Vishnu, has periodic
avatars. The world of *The Confidence-Man: His Masquerade*,
like the world of the Hindus, can be seen as a dialectic masquerade of the two conflicting forms—preservation and destruction, love and hate, confidence and delusion, white and
black, Vishnu and Siva. In both Hinduism and *The Confidence-
Man* these two forms are shapes of the same being, in fact all
forms are shapes of the same being, and all men partake of the
unity imaged visually in the god that seems many but is one.

In Vishnu's last avatar, which is to come, he will appear
with the attributes of Siva the Destroyer as Kalki, an armed
warrior, to end the final age of man, the present age, the Age
of Time, by destroying man. This may be both Guinea's
"ge'mman as is a sodjer" and what is hinted in the final sentence: "Something further may follow of this Masquerade."
And it may also explain why the last character introduced
into the book, in the final chapter, is a boy with "leopard-like
teeth," with a face that "wore such a polish of seasoned
grime, that his sloe-eyes sparkled from out it like lustrous
sparks in fresh coal," and clothed in a "red-flannel shirt."
For Siva often appears as "a smoke-coloured boy" whose
"teeth are as large as an ogre's," who appears "clothed in red
raiment," and who "destroys all, or ... absorbs all essences
into himself at last." When the boy winks at the Cosmopoli-

tan and asks, "is the wind East, d'ye think?", one may sense their final apocalyptic union.

Melville makes the Hindu vision of the apocalypse over-shadow the Christian vision, in which the armed Word of God vanquishes Satan. Christ in *The Confidence-Man* merges into Satan as the shape-shifting struggles and ulti-mate identity of Vishnu and Siva generate a world in which all objects and events become fictions, all men become in-distinguishable, all gods become the Confidence Man, sal-vation means destruction, and black is only another appear-ance of white. This vision, at first appearance so destructive, is in reality most creative. To experience and survive it is to be re-created.

CHAPTER 3

Moby Dick

READINGS ON
HERMAN MELVILLE

Moby Dick:
An Introduction

Tyrus Hillway

In a piece meant to be an introduction to *Moby Dick*,
Tyrus Hillway outlines the main themes of Melville's
greatest novel, including Ahab's rebellion against
God. Hillway concludes that Melville implicitly criticizes Ahab for defying destiny. Hillway was one of
the founders of the Melville Society in 1945. Author
of *Melville and the Whale*, he contributed a large
number of articles and reviews to periodicals in
American and English literature. His three-act play
Captain Ahab, based on *Moby Dick*, has been produced in Nantucket, Massachusetts. He has been
president of Mitchell College and has been on the
faculty of Colorado State College.

"I have written a wicked book, and feel spotless as the lamb,"
reported Herman Melville to his Berkshire friend and neigh-
bor Nathaniel Hawthorne after the completion of *Moby-Dick*
in 1851. Regarding the story as most people do—that is, as
the tale of an adventurous whale hunt in the South Seas—
one can hardly call *Moby-Dick* a wicked book. What, then,
did Melville mean in making such a statement? Attempts to
answer this question have resulted in some of the most fan-
ciful and complex writing ever to mar the pages of literary
criticism. Yet its meaning is clear, I think, not only in Melville's comments upon his own experiences as an author but
in the explanations which he provided within the book itself.

Typee and *Omoo*, his earliest novels of adventure, won
Melville an enthusiastic audience. That audience, however,
was quickly and rudely turned against him by his third
book, *Mardi*, a long and somewhat involved allegory of
ideas. The bitterness aroused in Melville by the unfavorable
reception of *Mardi* led him to exclaim to Hawthorne, "Truth

Tyrus Hillway, "A Preface to *Moby Dick*," in *"Moby-Dick": Centennial Essays*, edited for
the Melville Society (Dallas: Southern Methodist University Press, 1953). Reprinted by
permission of the author.

is the silliest thing under the sun. Try to get a living by Truth—and go to the Soup Societies!" Of his literary methods in writing *Moby-Dick* he said, "What I feel most moved to write, that is banned,—it will not pay. Yet, altogether, write the *other* way I cannot. So the product is a final hash, and all my books are botches."

What Melville wanted, of course, was to teach, to deal with moral and philosophical ideas. His readers preferred to be entertained. What evolved, in order to satisfy both reader and writer, was a compromise. For most readers, even today, *Moby-Dick* remains a story of wild adventure. For its author, as creative artist, it was a framework of narrative within which he could raise vital moral, social, religious, and philosophical questions. Those of his novels in which he did not exhaustively ponder such weighty questions he regarded as merely potboilers.

Moby-Dick must be recognized, first of all, for what it is—not only an adventure story, but a profound study of human character and human destiny. The great question which it raises is this: What have the gods to do with man?

AHAB

Captain Ahab, conveyor of the protests of mankind against the injustices of fate, represents one point of view that may be taken toward life. He reveals this, for example, in a conversation with the ship's carpenter on the *Pequod,* when he exclaims, "Thou art as unprincipled as the gods, and as much of a jack-of-all-trades."

"But I do not mean anything, sir," is the reply. "I do as I do."

"The gods again," says Ahab.

Here is the essence of his observations upon divine power. Struck and maimed by the whale, a brute beast of the sea, forced thus to suffer both physical and mental anguish, Ahab refuses to accept the suffering as his just lot. "Why was I singled out," he seems to cry, like so many moderns, "by fate or God for such torment?" His reaction is to roar defiance. If the gods take the liberty of striking him, he will strike back blow for blow. But where shall he strike? What visible form do the gods take? In the most powerful speech of the entire book, Ahab explains matters as follows to Starbuck, his first mate:

All visible objects, man, are but as pasteboard masks. But in each event—in the living act, the undoubted deed—there, some unknown but still reasoning thing puts forth the mouldings of its features from behind the unreasoning mask. If man will strike, strike through the mask! How can the prisoner reach outside except by thrusting through the wall? To me, the white whale is that wall, shoved near to me. Sometimes I think there's naught beyond. But 'tis enough. He tasks me; he heaps me; I see in him outrageous strength, with an inscrutable malice sinewing it. That inscrutable thing is chiefly what I hate; and be the white whale agent or be the white whale principal, I will wreak that hate upon him.

This tokens a kind of heroism, a Prometheanism, in Ahab. He voices the implied protest of all humanity. Yet Ahab is mad. If he utters in his mad raptures a few of the truths with malice in them which trouble saner minds, he is mad none the less. His tremendous power to work his will upon other men seems to be all the more heightened by the form of his insanity; but his futile and unreasonable feud with nature's brute forces, his deliberate courting of destruction, prove the wreck of his essential instruments of mental balance. Melville, of course, knew exactly what he was doing when he made Ahab mad. While he admired, he could not have approved Ahab's theories or his inhuman pride in applying them. Influenced, without any doubt, by his master Shakespeare, Melville created in Ahab a megalomaniac of the modern world.

One result of Ahab's madness is his isolation from the rest of humanity. Like Faust, he has bartered his immortal soul for the right to consider himself a demigod. Fedallah and his mysterious companions appear to be the guides appointed to conduct his soul to hell. In achieving his temporarily exalted status, Ahab, like Hawthorne's Ethan Brand, commits the unpardonable sin of pride and attempts to reject his kinship with other humankind. At more than one point in the story he actually senses the fact that by giving up his defiant quest he can regain his soul and return to sanity. The tragedy of the plot lies in his never quite managing to bring this about, even under the urgings of the kind and sensible Starbuck. His physical and spiritual separation from his wife and child, his disdain for the ordinary comforts of life, his destruction of the helpful quadrant—all these mark his withdrawal from the common level of mankind into an egocentric stratosphere between the world of man and the heaven of God. He remains the defier of fate.

WORSHIPING WITH THE PAGAN QUEEQUEG

In this scene from Moby-Dick, *Ishmael and the pagan Quee-queg spend the night in a rented room before setting sail the next day on the* Pequod. *Melville uses Ishmael, a rather shel-tered "good Christian," as the perfect foil to Queequeg's pagan worship. In a scene filled with irony and humor, Ish-mael ultimately concludes that it is a Christian act to wor-ship Queequeg's idol, an "insignificant bit of black wood."*

Wild he was; a very sight of sights to see; yet I began to feel myself mysteriously drawn towards him. And those same things that would have repelled most others, they were the very magnets that thus drew me. I'll try a pagan friend, thought I, since Christian kindness has proved but hollow courtesy. . . .

He made me a present of his embalmed head; took out his enormous tobacco wallet, and groping under the tobacco, drew out some thirty dollars in silver; then spreading them on the table, and mechanically dividing them into two equal portions, pushed one of them towards me, and said it was mine. I was going to remonstrate; but he silenced me by pouring them into my trowsers' pockets. I let them stay. He then went about his evening prayers, took out his idol, and removed the paper fireboard. By certain signs and symp-toms, I thought he seemed anxious for me to join him; but well knowing what was to follow, I deliberated a moment whether, in case he invited me, I would comply or otherwise.

I was a good Christian; born and bred in the bosom of the infallible Presbyterian Church. How then could I unite with this wild idolator in worshipping his piece of wood? But what is worship? thought I. Do you suppose now, Ishmael, that the magnanimous God of heaven and earth—pagans and all included—can possibly be jealous of an insignificant bit of black wood? Impossible! But what is worship?—to do the will of God—*that* is worship. And what is the will of God?—to do to my fellow man what I would have my fellow man to do to me—*that* is the will of God. Now, Queequeg is my fellow man. And what do I wish that this Queequeg would do to me? Why, unite with me in my particular Pres-byterian form of worship. Consequently, I must then unite with him in his; ergo, I must turn idolator. So I kindled the shavings; helped prop up the innocent little idol; offered him burnt biscuit with Queequeg; salaamed before him twice or thrice; kissed his nose; and that done, we un-dressed and went to bed, at peace with our own consciences and all the world.

PIP

"Oh, ye frozen heavens! look down here," shouts Ahab, observing Pip. "Ye did beget this luckless child and have abandoned him, ye creative libertines." Pip, too, is insane.

Pip, as a matter of fact, constitutes Ahab's foil. A small and cowardly Negro lad, he loses his mind when cast adrift for several hours on the wild and open sea. But the important thing about Pip is that he makes no real protest against his fate. He is at the opposite pole of Ahab's axis. His pathetic figure stirs in Ahab his most disturbing feelings of kinship with humanity. So disturbing to Ahab are these feelings that he consciously resists them, although Pip's influence nearly succeeds in saving him. Pip's reactions to life are almost all passive, and he provides for Ahab a means of salvation by giving him something human to protect and help. Unfortunately, Ahab's pride is never completely mastered by Pip's humility.

STARBUCK

While Pip touches Ahab's heart, Starbuck touches his reason. Starbuck, like a good angel, gradually draws Ahab away from his evil purpose—but too late. Ahab, well aware that Starbuck has common sense in his favor, resists him first by reasoning, then by threats. Even though almost overwhelmed by the force of Ahab's personality, Starbuck holds to his convictions and sets out to save both Ahab and the crew. At one point, convinced of his captain's madness, he is ready to assassinate him in order to preserve the others from being drawn into tragedy with him; yet this contemplated violent act proves too strong for Starbuck's good principles. He cannot force himself to commit murder and returns to the only weapon at his command—reason.

Melville wrote to his friend Hawthorne with some bravado that the secret motto of *Moby-Dick* might be found in Ahab's consecration of the harpoon: *Ego non baptizo te in nomine patris, sed in nomine diaboli* [I baptize thee not in the name of the Father, but in the name of the Devil]. It seems clear, however, that Melville was being more than half humorous in this declaration. A more likely motto can be discovered, I believe, in one of the two important sermons which are preached in the book. One sermon is delivered by the Negro cook on the *Pequod* to the sharks, comparing them in greed and rapacity with men. The other is the beautiful and moving discourse of Father Mapple in the chapel at New

Bedford, on the theme of Jonah. The following words from Father Mapple's great sermon form a motto which is nearer, I think, to Melville's intention in *Moby-Dick* than any other which might be selected:

> All the things that God would have us do are hard for us to do—remember that—and hence, he oftener commands us than endeavors to persuade. And if we obey God, we must disobey ourselves; and it is in this disobeying ourselves, wherein the hardness of obeying God consists.

Here we have Ahab's case exactly. That godless, god-like man has taken the whale's attack upon him as a personal affront, and he consequently blames God for creating a world in which brotherhood is preached while vulturism is practiced.

"Faith? What's that?" cries Ahab derisively, in his bitterness. Yet there rings a hollowness in the cry. Struggle and fume as he will, he cannot escape the suspicion that even his defiance of God is preordained. Perhaps that thought serves to add something to his exasperation. He unhesitatingly accepts Fedallah's prophecies, of course, and so shows himself a fatalist. In the face of nearly certain annihilation he pauses briefly to justify himself by asserting, "I am the Fates' lieutenant; I act under orders."

Perhaps too much has already been written about Melville's powerful symbolism. From the literary point of view, his language is unusually colorful and rich with symbolical import. His use of symbols, however, has led many to look for hidden meanings of all kinds in his works. For the most part, I think, his intentions are plain to see. While it is true that Melville, for fear of losing his readers, may have attempted to clothe his ideas in allegory in order to avoid the shock of the naked thought, I feel sure that his fondness for the symbol came from a natural predilection in which he took a literary delight. He seldom lost an opportunity to turn a physical fact into an artistic device. For this he had to await appreciation until the twentieth century.

The conclusion remains that *Moby-Dick* must be recognized as much less a tale of maritime adventure than a novel of ideas and spiritual conflict. The great White Whale, with all his majesty and frightfulness, becomes inevitably the symbol of a universal power (or its mask) which Ahab feels to be unjust and against which he rebels. The effect of Ahab's mad rebellion upon himself and upon those who surround him, and not the hazards of the chase, however interesting these may be, constitutes the story's theme.

This theme the America of the present century can at last understand. In Melville's own day, engrossed in political and economic expansion, the American public almost angrily rejected any suggestion that it should examine rationally the relation of the individual to his universe, especially when such an examination might weaken some established institutions of considerable popular influence. It was mainly upon the appeal of a direct practical application that an idea could hope to win many followers. We are now willing to listen to Melville because, having exhausted our energies in expansionism and having finally reached a point of disillusionment, we have again become interested in the meaning of man. When the nation was rapt in its great work of colonization and construction, there was little time for such thinking. Truth could be doled out, as it were, by the professionals and accepted substantially without scrutiny.

Even the long struggle between the church and science took place during the nineteenth century on a somewhat superficial plane. Except in the later phases, it resembled less a clash between opposing views of true teaching than a struggle for influence between factions. The underlying contradictions—where faith enters the picture for both religion and science—were only dimly discerned; and the battle raged chiefly over "authorities" and "evidence." As the scientific discoveries placed new emphasis upon the material and rational factors in human life, those who recognized the basic issues were deeply moved. Among these Melville may be numbered; for Melville was habitually one who dived deep. Religious in the sense that he believed instinctively in the need for a firm faith, scientific in the sense that he accepted no dogma without clear evidence, he saw reluctantly the futility of seeking final truth. The knowledge of our common limitation in this respect seems to have aggravated in him the festering of a restless frustration. Emotionally, he hungered for faith, but he could not accept it blindly.

Something of his perplexity pervades the pages of *Moby-Dick*, his masterpiece. Few answers, many questions. Above all, the tragic question: What have the gods to do with man? Whatever the correct answer may be, we know that Ahab's was the wrong one. To rebel against one's destiny, to defy God, leads only, it is clear, to tragedy.

Melville's Use of Greek Myth in *Moby Dick*

Gerard M. Sweeney

Herman Melville uses allegory; literary, mythological, and biblical references; and other devices to reveal layers of meaning in his works. In this article, Gerard M. Sweeney focuses on Melville's use of Greek mythology; specifically, he compares Ahab, the captain of the *Pequod* in *Moby Dick*, to Prometheus, who steals fire from the gods to bring it to humanity. Sweeney claims that Melville patterned Ahab after Prometheus, and that by understanding the parallels we can more deeply understand Ahab's character and, ultimately, *Moby Dick* as a whole. Critic Gerard M. Sweeney is the author of the book *Melville's Use of Classical Mythology*.

No matter how the Romantics interpreted Prometheus, no matter how they transformed and re-created him into a heroic and humanitarian savior, unjustly tortured by a despotic tyrant, an attentive reading of *Prometheus Bound* reveals that Aeschylus conceived of his hero as a flawed sinner. Certainly he deserved admiration because of his fearlessness and massive will, but he was nevertheless a criminal, one who had sinned and who kept on sinning, one who underwent his deserved punishment with continued defiance and unregeneracy. "From Aeschylus to Calderon," according to Lewis Awad, "the role Prometheus played in the cosmos, regardless of our attitude toward that role, implied a high degree of sinfulness for which he was bound and from which he needed to be delivered.". . .

AHAB'S CRIME

[Melville] could not have read Aeschylus' *Prometheus* without recognizing—although perhaps admiring as well—the

From *Melville's Use of Classical Mythology* by Gerard M. Sweeney. Copyright 1975 Editions Rodopi N.V., Amsterdam. Reprinted by permission of the author.

fatal depravity in the heart of its hero. And this is precisely what the reader of *Moby-Dick* must grant Melville: that he had read his Aeschylus perceptively, that he knew who Prometheus was and what he was, and that, when he established the numerous connections between Prometheus and Ahab, he did so in full awareness of the Titan's flawed nature.

Prometheus and Ahab are both criminals. Prometheus stole, as Strength reminds Vulcan in the opening lines of *Prometheus Bound,*

> Thy radiant pride, the fiery flame, that lends
> Its aid to every art . . . and bore
> The gift to mortals; for which bold offence
> The gods assign him this just punishment;
> That he may learn to reverence the power
> Of Jove, and moderate his love to man.

The accusation capsules not only the specific crime of Prometheus, but also the character flaws underlying the crime: immoderation, or a failure to recognize and accept his limitations; and a willful disrespect for the deity. . . . One should note too that Prometheus' crime illustrates not merely his sinful defiance; it suggests as well, as C. Kerenyi claims [in *Prometheus*], a defect in his own being. "The theft of fire—because it is a theft—characterizes the thief as one whose existence is inherently deficient. . . . Neither Hephaistos nor Hermes had any need to steal fire. The darkness of Prometheus signifies precisely the deficiency of one who needs fire in order to achieve a more perfect form of being. In obtaining this higher form of being for man, Prometheus shows himself to be man's double, an eternal image of man's basically imperfect form of being." Ahab's crime consists in his defiant attempt to annihilate Moby Dick, a crime which, even on its surface, is comparable to the mythic theft of fire. For one thing the very business of whaling constitutes a theft of fire. Involving, as a number of readers have noted, the exploitation of nature, its goal is to obtain for men the sperm whale's oil, the fuel for their flames. Then too, the particular pursuit of the White Whale is significantly described by Ishmael as "the fiery hunt"; that it represents a conflict with a deity—such as Zeus or Jupiter—is made clear by the numerous references to Moby Dick as a god.

More importantly, one episode of *Moby-Dick*—the typhoon scene in "The Candles"—seems to be Melville's intentional re-creation of the mythic theft of fire. Prometheus' theft, as he describes it [in *Prometheus Bound*], was accomplished by the stealthy hiding of the divine spark in a fennel stalk.

> For favours shown
> To mortal man I bear this weight of woe;
> Hid in a hollow cane the fount of fire
> I privately conveyed, of every art
> Productive, and the noblest gift to men.

Ahab's "theft," in contrast, is a boldly defiant deed, set amidst elemental nature in furious eruption. (The setting much resembles the stark desolation of Aeschylus' Caucasus, the mountain on which Prometheus is chained, as it explodes with the wrath of Zeus.) The scene depicts corpusants settling on the *Pequod*'s masts, transforming each into a gigantic candle. Hereupon Ahab, his foot resting on the bowed Parsee, grasps the lightning chains. Then, as if dramatically responding to Ahab, the lightning attaches itself to his harpoon, "and from the keen steel barb there now came a levelled flame of pale, forked fire." Immediately Starbuck interprets the omen to signify divine disapproval and frantically begs Ahab to order an end to the voyage.

> Overhearing Starbuck, the panic-stricken crew instantly ran to the braces—though not a sail was left aloft. For the moment all the aghast mate's thoughts seemed theirs; they raised a half-mutinous cry. But dashing the rattling lightning links to the deck, and snatching the burning harpoon, Ahab waved it like a torch among them; swearing to transfix with it the first sailor that but cast loose a rope's end. Petrified by his aspect, and still more shrinking from the fiery dart that he held, the men fell back in dismay, and Ahab again spoke:

> "All your oaths to hunt the White Whale are as binding as mine; and heart, soul, and body, lungs and life, old Ahab is bound. And that ye may know to what tune this heart beats; look ye here; thus I blow out the last fear!" And with one blast of his breath he extinguished the flame.

In Ahab's grabbing the lightning chains and especially in his waving the fiery harpoon—in a way emblematic of all his actions—the reader should see Melville's modified equivalent of Prometheus' smuggling from heaven the fire-laden fennel stalk. It is a striking allusion, one which attests the degree to which Melville was thinking of Prometheus while shaping his conception of Ahab. Perhaps unconsciously, perhaps as a clue to the reader, Melville has Ahab admit he is "bound." (Four chapters later Starbuck will consider, but reject, the idea of binding Ahab in his cabin, and Fedallah will last be seen bound to the White Whale, foreshadowing Ahab's descent to the depths, also tied to Moby Dick.)

Ahab's fire-grabbing re-creates not only the external crime of Prometheus, but the internal crime as well. For although Prometheus' intention is to benefit men, while Ahab's is to coerce them, the essence of both heroes' actions is criminal defiance of the deity. As he addresses the corpusants, Ahab states his case against the god he originally worshipped in the form of fire. "Oh! thou clear spirit of clear fire, whom on these seas I as Persian once did worship, till in the sacramental act so burned by thee, that to this hour I bear the scar; I now know thee, thou clear spirit, and I now know that thy right worship is defiance.". . .

THE HUBRIS OF AHAB AND PROMETHEUS

Not only do Prometheus and Ahab believe they know the mind and workings of the powers above, they also propose to alter or reverse the supernatural design, and herein lies the acme of their tragic hubris. Erroneously convinced that Zeus planned the destruction of man, Prometheus stole fire in order to contravene the will of the god. (And even if Zeus had intended man's annihilation, the crime of Prometheus would still be the same.) His theft exemplified his fatal pride, and his continued refusal to obey the god, to give him the information he desires, is another manifestation of his defiant hubris. . . .

Ahab is infected with colossal pride. He reveals it in thinking that his intellect can penetrate the mystery of evil and even more so in thinking that, by killing Moby Dick, he can expel evil from the cosmos. Starbuck recognizes Ahab's hubris when he calls his goal "blasphemous," a "heaven-insulting purpose." Ishmael notes it too when he surveys Ahab after he has turned the ominously inverted compass needle: "In his fiery eyes of scorn and triumph, you then saw Ahab in all his fatal pride." And Ahab himself admits he is "proud as a Greek god," an admission that makes his pride even greater than Prometheus', since, while Ahab is merely a man, his classical counterpart was in fact a demi-deity. Moreover, Ahab's recognition of his hubris increases his culpability, since, instead of extirpating the sin, he glories in it.

Because of their hubristic activities, both heroes are accused of madness. The Chorus warns Prometheus not to let his love of man "o'erleap the bounds/ Of reason," but he persists in his rebellion, even when Mercury arrives to undertake a final attempt to make him relent.

> MER. Thy malady, I find, is no small madness.
> PRO. If to detest my enemies be madness,
>   It is a malady I wish to have.
> MER. Were it well with thee, who could brook thy pride?

Finally the messenger exclaims, totally frustrated with the Titan's continued defiance,

> Such ravings, such wild counsels might you hear
> From moon-struck madness. What is this but madness?

. . . Ahab's madness lies in a comparable dissociation from reality—the inscrutable reality of the White Whale—and it is therefore connected with his hubris; it involves his attempting to achieve a goal that is supernatural, that is beyond the limits set in reality for mortal man. So to Starbuck Ahab is "a madman," and his pursuit of Moby Dick is "madness." To Ishmael he is "crazy Ahab." And just as he recognizes his excessive pride, Ahab also realizes he is mad. "I'm demoniac," he soliloquizes, "I'm madness maddened!". . .

WARNINGS

Both heroes, moreover, hear a number of direct verbal warnings, Prometheus from the Chorus, and Ahab from Starbuck. Although Prometheus receives explicit reproofs from Oceanus, as well as threats from Mercury and outright abuse from Strength and Force, the choric admonitions are the strongest, from the reader's point of view, since the Chorus sincerely sympathizes with the sufferings of the hero. . . .

ISHMAEL: THE IDEAL SPECTATOR

A number of critics have noted that Ishmael serves a chronic function in *Moby-Dick*. He is akin to the playwright's "ideal spectator," being on the stage throughout the tragedy (like the Greek chorus), observing and commenting on the conflict and the characters. His ever-present voice offers in this sense the narrative equivalent of the dramatic chorus. Ishmael also serves another traditional choric function by providing the audience with relevant factual information: background information on Ahab and discussions of cetology. More importantly, Ishmael is, like the Chorus of *Prometheus Bound*, sympathetic with the hero. In fact for a time he is even an accessory to Ahab's crime, having sworn with the others the blasphemous oath. Nonetheless, he is not completely caught up in Ahab's insanity: Melville wants us to be certain of this. Although Ishmael does take the oath—which he later formally rejects—he takes it in "the abandonment of the time and the place." Moreover, his reasons for battling Moby Dick are not Ahab's reasons. It is not the incarnate evil, but "The Whiteness of the Whale" that most appalls Ishmael. It is a reaction which he feels only "at times"—at other times he lauds the godlike and majestic beauty of the whale—and which, he painstakingly points out, is a common human and animal response. Thus while he sympathizes with and even praises Ahab, Ishmael can, like the Chorus of the *Prometheus,* frequently censure the hero. Furthermore, the narrator's philosophy seems to be most equatable with the author's. Ishmael's acceptance of the White Whale's inscrutability and of the mysteries that are ultimately unsolvable and his consequent acceptance of life's tragic nature appear to be Melville's. This of course is not to deny that Melville accepts these things reluctantly or that Ishmael's sympathy for Ahab—which is so intimately connected with his criticism—is not Melville's as well. . . .

AHAB'S PUNISHMENT

Melville was so influenced by the Aeschylean Prometheus story that he allusively linked Ahab's career not only to the crimes of the Titan, but to the punishments as well. Prometheus' punishment is a triple one, the first part occurring as the play opens when the Titan is chained to the rock. The second and third stages begin at the end of the play and are outlined to the hero by Mercury, threatening the protagonist for the last time.

> But mark me well,
> If not obedient to my words, a storm,
> A fiery and inevitable deluge
> Shall burst in threefold vengeance on thy head.
> First, his fierce thunder winged with lightning flames
> Shall rend this rugged rock, and cover thee
> With hideous ruin: long time shall thou lie
> Astonied in its rifted sides, till dragged
> Again to light; then shall the bird of Jove,
> The rav'ning eagle, lured with scent of blood,
> Mangle thy body, and each day returning,
> An uninvited guest, plunge his fell beak,
> And feast and riot on thy black'ning liver.

Ahab's punishment is clearly structured on Prometheus', but it is chronologically reversed: first he is attacked by Melville's equivalent of the Aeschylean "bird of Jove," and then he is sent to the lower depths, from which, unlike Prometheus, he will never rise.

Central to Melville's implicit comparison of the two punishments is the bird imagery which begins with Ishmael's description of Moby Dick appearing on the first day of the chase accompanied by "hundreds of gay fowl." "Like to some flag-staff rising from the painted hull of an argosy, the tall but shattered pole of a recent lance projected from the white whale's back; and at intervals one of the cloud of soft-toed fowls hovering, and to and from skimming like a canopy over the fish, silently perched and rocked on this pole, the long tail feathers streaming like pennons." Shortly later, "the grand god revealed himself, sounded, and went out of sight," and "the white sea-fowls lovingly lingered over the agitated pool that he left." An hour after this, anticipating Moby Dick's return to the surface, the birds begin "fluttering over the water ... wheeling round and round, with joyous, expectant cries." To enforce the point that these birds constitute a royal entourage of the Whale-as-Zeus, Melville explicitly links Moby Dick to the god by alluding to "the white bull Jupiter swimming away with ravished Europa." Other birds furnish still more specific correspondences. A red-billed sea-hawk—which seems Melville's equivalent of the "rav'ning eagle" of Jove—rips Ahab's hat from his head, and then another (or more likely the same one returning as the classical bird periodically returns) tears away the red flag flying from the ship's main mast. Ahab ironically links himself to the punishment of Prometheus by describing the Parsee's disappearance on the second day of the chase as "a riddle" that pecks his brain "like a hawk's beak." And finally, in light of the previous bird imagery, one should note the sharks that trail Ahab's boat on the last day. They follow "in the same prescient way that vultures hover over the banners of marching regiments in the east." Molesting none of the others, they pursue Ahab's boat alone, snapping at the oars.

Melville's repeated references to attacking birds of prey are doubtless intended to recall the punishment of Prometheus. But they should also remind us that Ahab suffers, like the Greek hero, from a recurring wound. The sufferings of Ahab and Prometheus are unlike those of other tragic heroes, such as Euripides' Pentheus or Sophocles' Ajax, who undergo a single punishment for a single crime. In contrast to these first offenders, Prometheus and Ahab are punished by repeated assaults that are consistent with their careers of unregenerate pride and defiance. The liver of Prometheus is eaten; then it regrows and is eaten again. Since the liver is considered the seat of the very passions which the hero permits to overrule his reason, the cyclical punishment is a fit emblem of his unregeneracy. The symbolic function of Ahab's leg wound is similar. He is dismasted once in his first encounter with Moby Dick; then on shore he breaks the ivory replacement; he later weakens the false leg when recklessly leaving the *Samuel Enderby*, having just received an additional warning from another amputee; and finally he again breaks the ivory replacement in his encounter with Moby Dick on the second day of the chase. Ahab's recurring leg wounds—considered with the fact that he still feels the pain of the absent limb—should be seen as Melville's equivalent of the wounded liver of Prometheus, eaten, regrown, and eaten again. Finally one should note that, while Ahab's on-shore injury clearly has sexual overtones, it also seems Melville's re-creation of an additional wound of Prometheus. Ahab's fall on shore so displaced his ivory leg that "it had *stake-wise smitten*, and all but pierced his groin." The allusive significance of this wound strikes the reader when he recalls that when Prometheus is chained to the rock he is further tormented by having a stake driven through his chest.

While Prometheus' punishment begins with his descent and Ahab's ends with his, the two descents—each being the catastrophe of the respective tragedy—are equatable in light of the context of each work. Prometheus is sent to Tartarus bound to his rock, just as Ahab sinks below the waves tied to the White Whale. In each tragedy, moreover, the hero's associates accompany him in his descent to the depths. The wrath of Zeus being imminent, the Chorus of the *Prometheus* is explicitly warned by Mercury to "remove with speed" from the scene.

> Remember you are warned; if ill o'ertake you
> Accuse not Fortune, lay not the blame on Jove,
> As by his hand sunk in calamities
> Unthought of, unforeseen: no, let the blame
> Light on yourselves; your folly not unwarned,
> Not unawares, but 'gainst your better knowledge,
> Involved you in th' inextricable toils.

The crew of the *Pequod* has received similar warnings, since they have witnessed the same omens and heard the same admonitions that Ahab has. Indeed, knowing the *Town-Ho's* tale of Radney and Steelkilt—a story Ahab is ignorant of— the crew has in fact received an additional warning. So like Aeschylus' Chorus, they sink into calamities that are not unforeseen. This is especially true of Starbuck, who performs so many of the choric functions. More than any of the others Starbuck is acting against his better knowledge. His better knowledge—or his reliable intuition—informs him, as he handles the musket outside Ahab's door, that "come to deadly harm, my soul swears this ship will, if Ahab have his way." But he refuses to act, and therefore the blame is partially his as he sinks, caught in the catastrophe of his Promethean captain.

From both tragedies, however, there exits a single wandering survivor, each of whom suggests a modicum of promise. Io will suffer the torments of the gadfly, but eventually she will settle and conceive a new race, the thirteenth descendent of which will be Hercules, who will free Prometheus from his chains (probably with the permission of Zeus and after some form of reconciliation between the Titan and the god). The promise embodied in Ishmael is that he attains a tragic acceptance, an acceptance which Ahab cannot reach. At the opening of *Moby-Dick*, as Bruce Franklin states, in "Hawthorne and Melville: The Unpardonable Sin," "Ishmael . . . is Ahab in miniature, isolated, defiant, obsessed. But, unlike Ahab, Ishmael changes in the course of the novel; the experience of the sea becomes for him an experience of purgation, purification." Like Noah—and like Deucalion, the son of Prometheus—Ishmael escapes the watery catastrophe which must be viewed as something like a deity's wrathful punishment of an impious man and his cohorts. But before he escapes Ishmael, like Io, suffers. Because of his involvement in Ahab's crime he is sucked into the black abyss, but is released just before the ultimate descent. So for the moments before his release, spinning in the vortex of the sinking *Pequod*, he is "like another Ixion," one of the few Greek sinners who, like Prometheus, was crucified.

Hindu Mythology in *Moby Dick*

H.B. Kulkarni

While Melville's use of Western mythology, especially
Greek and Roman myth and the Bible, has been
noted by many authors, H.B. Kulkarni argues that an
understanding of Hindu mythology is equally impor-
tant in reading *Moby Dick*. In the following article,
Kulkarni argues that Melville was very familiar with
contemporary works on Hinduism, and peppered
Moby Dick with references to the tradition in order to
elevate the novel into a "symbolic quest for God and
Truth." Kulkarni is the author of *Moby Dick: A Hindu
Avatar: A Study of Hindu Myth and Thought in Moby
Dick*, from which this article is excerpted.

Melville's references to Hindu myth and thought, however
peripheral to his works some have thought them to be, are
so numerous that there can be no doubt about his extensive
knowledge of Hinduism. The depth of his understanding,
however, has not been sufficiently explored.

"The only extant account of Melville as an academic student of Oriental mythologies," as James Baird points out, is
to be found in the memoirs of Maunsell Field. Field reports
Melville's conversation with Oliver Wendell Holmes on the
religions and mythologies of India, when he visited Melville
with his friend Darley in the summer of 1855:

> At length, somehow, the conversation drifted to East India re-
> ligions and mythologies, and soon there arose a discussion
> between Holmes and Melville, which was conducted with the
> most amazing skill and brilliancy on both sides. It lasted for
> hours and Darley and I had nothing to do but listen.

Though it is the only account, it is strong testimony for Melville's knowledge of India's religion and mythology.

Howard P. Vincent was, perhaps, the first to raise the
question about Melville's sources of such information,

specifically about Vishnu and his *Matse-Avatar*, mentioned in *Moby-Dick*: "Where did Melville learn about the Matse Avatar, as he called it in chapter 55, or about Vishnu in general?" Although Vincent knows that "a complete answer to this question seems impossible," he suggests and offers some evidence that Melville must have read *Indian Antiquities* (7 volumes) and *History of Hindostan* (3 volumes) by Reverend Thomas Maurice. It is also certain that Melville was familiar with the works of Sir William Jones, who was the first President of the Royal Society of Bengal and Calcutta and was a major promoter of scholarship and research in Asiatic life and letters. Melville mentions him by name in *Moby-Dick* and refers to his knowledge of thirty languages. His acquaintance with the works of these scholars is confirmed by Merton Sealts in his careful compilation of Melville's library.

But going beyond such specifics, it is certain that Melville would not have needed to go out of his way for information on the exotic East. Orientalism was indeed one of the major preoccupations of scholarship in Melville's time, and after the European mastery of Sanskrit and the establishment of correspondence among Indo-European languages, the reading world of America received a generous supply of books, pamphlets, and articles on India and the various aspects of its life and thought. Poole's *Index to Periodical Literature* of the first half of the nineteenth century lists thousands of items on India, Hindu mythology and religion, and allied matter. If this material did not form part of the regular diet of the common American, a sensitive and alert mind like Melville could not have missed encountering it in his normal reading of books and magazines:

> Melville was a voracious reader and he turned to books, magazines, newspapers as an experience, in their relevance to his art, equal to participation and observation; pictures impressed him as deeply as words. He used books for their music as well as for their ideas and information.

Recent critics of Melville seem to be in general agreement on Melville's extensive knowledge of Eastern mythology and religion:

> Melville read widely in the popular sources of mythology—modern periodicals and ancient and modern poetry, fiction, drama, and travel literature. He also read deeply in the central documents of the post-Renaissance mythology—the ponderous polemical tomes of learned heretics and divines. It

has been shown that Melville used as sources, for instance, an English translation of Bayle's *Dictionnaire* and the Reverend Thomas Maurice's *Indian Antiquities.*

Perhaps Melville's reading was neither scholarly nor academic. But it was definitely creative:

> As a man who had barely finished high school, he developed an extraordinary ability to extract the essence of ideas from slight intimations, assimilating his reading with an imaginative intensity not often to be found among "trained minds."

This study, then, assuming Melville's genuine interest in and more than adequate knowledge of Hindu myth and thought, will attempt to demonstrate that the vast amount of information which he picked up in his discursive reading sank into his mind and was transformed into a kind of feeling for things Oriental, which, instead of distorting facts, illuminated them with a native flavor that, perhaps, only a person born into the tradition can sense and understand. James Baird recognises this feeling in Melville, though he identifies it simply in broad terms as a genuine feeling for Primitivism which, he thinks, informs his symbols and makes his works a supreme example of Primitive Art. Baird is convinced that Melville had "an obsession with the primeval East." Melville's interest in Eastern mythology cannot be explained in terms of idle curiosity or desire for exotic novelty, for it is deeply embedded in his intense spiritual questioning and is an integral part of his artistic discipline looking for fresh and appropriate symbols as correlatives of his life's vision. Melville's quest can be understood in the light of Whitman's "Passage to India," for he may be described, in his own words, as a "thought diver" who strives to "*eclaircise* the myths Asiatic, the primitive fables" and in his exploration sounds "below the Sanscrit and the Vedas."

In recent years there have been some significant publications investigating in depth Melville's use of Oriental mythology. Among them, *The Wake of the Gods* by H. Bruce Franklin, *Melville's Orienda* by Dorothee Metlisky Finkelstein, and *Ishmael* by James Baird, referred to earlier, may be mentioned. . . .

In Melville, symbols taken from different mythologies of the world are set side by side with Biblical allusions. Sometimes they merge into one another. One does not eliminate the other, but they all by their juxtaposition, superimposition, and subtle interaction achieve a tremendous extension of metaphysical signification few narratives achieve. Melville presents a supreme example of mythological synthesis accomplished not by elimination but by assimilation of what appears to be its opposite. Did he not celebrate the marriage of a cannibal with a Christian at the very opening of *Moby-Dick* and direct the reader into this channel of synthesis? . . .

KEY PASSAGES ON HINDU MYTH

It is necessary at the very beginning of this study to take cognizance of the objections critics have raised against the relevance of Hindu myth to the structure and significance of *Moby-Dick*. Most critics have noted what may be called the key passages of Hindu myth, but they are either indifferent to them or feel unconcerned about their importance. That Melville should give a fairly detailed description of the story of Vishnu in two places is itself an indication that he did not intend it to be read and forgotten. While trying to present the "true form of this whale," he adverts to those "curious imaginary portraits of him" and describes the Hindu whale as the most ancient portrait available in the world:

> Now, by all odds, the most ancient extant portrait anyways purporting to be the whale's is to be found in the famous cavern pagoda of Elephanta, in India. The Brahmins maintain that in the almost endless sculptures of that immemorial pagoda, all the trades and pursuits, every conceivable avocation of man, were prefigured ages before any of them actually came into being. No wonder then, that in some sort our noble profession of whaling should have been there shadowed forth. The Hindoo whale referred to, occurs in a separate department of the wall, depicting the incarnation of Vishnu in the form of leviathan, learnedly known as the Matse Avatar.

In addition to this reference to the portrait of the Hindu leviathan at Elephanta, Melville mentions the context in which Vishnu incarnates himself as a fish and relates him to the whalemen's fraternity:

> That wondrous oriental story is now to be rehearsed from the Shaster which gives us the dread Vishnoo, one of the three persons in the godhead of the Hindoos; gives us this divine Vishnoo himself for our Lord:—Vishnoo, who, by the first of his ten earthly incarnations, has forever set apart and sanctified the whale. When Brahma, or the God of Gods saith the Shaster, resolved to recreate the world after one of its periodical dissolutions, he gave birth to Vishnoo, to preside over the work; but the Vedas, or mystical books, whose perusal would seem to have been indispensable to Vishnoo before beginning the creation, and which therefore must have contained some-

thing in the shape of practical hints to young architects, these Vedas were lying at the bottom of the waters; so Vishnu became incarnate in a whale, and sounding down in him to the utter-most depths, rescued the sacred volumes. Was not this Vishnoo a whalemen, then? even as a man who rides a horse is called a horseman?

... A close study of these passages shows that Melville was

THE SIGNIFICANCE OF WHITENESS

In the chapter "The Whiteness of the Whale," Ishmael gives a laundry list of the world's mythologies and how they all revere the color white, yet ends with the ways in which white is also terrifying. This excerpt gives just a sampling of Melville's extensive knowledge of world mythologies.

Whiteness has been even made significant of gladness, for among the Romans a white stone marked a joyful day; ... though even in the higher mysteries of the most august religions it has been made the symbol of the divine spotlessness and power; by the Persian fire worshippers, the white forked flame being held the holiest on the altar; and in the Greek mythologies, Great Jove himself being made incarnate in a snow-white bull; and though to the noble Iroquois, the mid-winter sacrifice of the sacred White Dog was by far the holiest festival of their theology, that spotless, faithful creature being held the purest envoy they could send to the Great Spirit with the annual tidings of their own fidelity; and though directly from the Latin word for white, all Christian priests derive the name of one part of their sacred vesture, the alb or tunic, worn beneath the cassock; ... yet for all these accumulated associations, with whatever is sweet, and honorable, and sublime, there yet lurks an elusive something in the innermost idea of this hue, which strikes more of panic to the soul than that redness which affrights in blood.

This elusive quality it is, which causes the thought of whiteness, when divorced from more kindly associations, and coupled with any object terrible in itself, to heighten that terror to the furthest bounds. Witness the white bear of the poles, and the white shark of the tropics; what but their smooth, flaky whiteness makes them the transcendent horrors they are? That ghastly whiteness it is which imparts such an abhorrent mildness, even more loathsome than terrific, to the dumb gloating of their aspect. So that not the fierce-fanged tiger in his heraldic coat can so stagger courage as the white-shrouded bear or shark.

familiar with numerous details regarding the Hindu myth which he weaves so skillfully into the design of his novel. . . .

MELVILLE'S RIDICULE OF HINDU MYTH

H. Bruce Franklin's major objection to Hindu myth is based on Melville's ridicule of it in the chapter entitled "Monstrous Pictures of Whales." He states with unqualified emphasis:

> Melville's obvious ridicule of the Vishnu myth should be sufficient to discourage identification of Moby Dick with Vishnu. Indeed, Melville makes it clear that Vishnu is not to be taken as any fish at all.

But obviously Franklin has missed the whole point of Melville's ridicule. It is clear even in casual reading that Melville's ridicule is aimed not at any particular myth, Hindu or Christian, but at what he calls "this whole blundering business" of picturing the whale. What Melville is clearly suggesting is that all pictorial representations of the whale are "monstrous," for no one can ever paint the whale accurately. Many have tried and all have failed, and the Egyptian is no exception. The Hindus, the Egyptians, the Greeks, the Christians, the professionals, the non-professionals, the artists, and even those who claim to be scientists have all been victims of what Melville so aptly describes as "pictorial delusions":

> It may be that the primal source of all those pictorial delusions will be found among the oldest Hindoo, *Egyptian* [my italics], and Grecian sculptures. For ever since those inventive but unscrupulous times . . . something of the same sort of license prevailed, not only in most popular pictures of the whale, but in many scientific presentations of him."

Melville elaborates upon the manifold mistakes made in the depiction of the whale and finally concludes by saying:

> For all these reasons, then, anyway you may look at it, you must needs conclude that the great Leviathan is the one creature in the world which must remain unpainted to the last. True, one portrait may hit the mark much nearer than another, but none can hit it with any very considerable degree of exactness. So there is no earthly way of finding out what the whale really looks like.

It is clear that Melville's intention in this chapter on "Monstrous Pictures of Whales" is not to condemn the Hindu and Christian myths in order to commend and uphold the Egyptian myth, as Mr. Franklin would persuade us to believe, but to show how all earthly attempts at picturing the whale, including the Egyptian, are at best "authentic abortions of the truth."

The impossibility of accurate description of the whale is an idea that persists through the novel. In the chapter on "Cetology," he underscores the idea:

> As yet, however, the sperm whale, scientific or poetic, lives not complete in any literature. Far above other hunted whales, his is an unwritten life.

Franklin makes much of the comic tone with which Melville describes the Vishnu myth and calls it "obvious ridicule." The lighthearted bantering tone of Melville which plays delicately upon most of the serious concerns of the novel deserves better approach than such quick disposal in terms like "ridicule." It is a complex technique aimed not at the thing "ridiculed," but at directing the reader's attention to some underlying significance. Here the comic technique is used to emphasize the metaphysical subtlety and cosmic amplitude of the Leviathan which naturally eludes the grasp of the painter's brush, the sculptor's chisel, or the poet's tongue. Behind the half-serious pose which Melville takes and the comic edge of many of his observations is the suggestive method of poetry, which achieves extension of meaning not by logic or rational argument but by psychological association. Therefore what takes the reader to the Egyptian myth is the very path of nuances and suggestions which can open the door to Vishnu myth and associate both of them to *Moby-Dick*. The solution does not really lie in exclusion but in inclusion which is, perhaps, a better approach to analysing the complex structure of the novel. . . .

VISHNU AND MOBY DICK

Franklin continues his objections to identifying Moby Dick with Vishnu by stating:

> In the Hindu myth, the fish incarnates the preserving power. Moby Dick is the Destroyer, and Melville's precise ridicule of the Matse Avatar forestalls any mythological mitigation of this fact.

As the question of ridicule has been satisfactorily answered, the problem of Vishnu being the preserving power may be considered. It is true that the common notion about Vishnu is that his function is to preserve. But he incarnates himself on earth in order to destroy evil and save the world from degeneration and ruin. The fish-incarnation is the first of Vishnu's ten incarnations, each of which is specifically undertaken to destroy the evil forces of the world. Moreover, in India destruction and creation are not regarded as exclusive terms at all. Wisdom lies in recognising the basic paradox of life, wherein destruction itself is creative. Maurice recognises the true spirit of India's philosophy and religion, when he says: "According to the philosophy of India, 'to *destroy* is only to *generate* and *reproduce* in another way.'"

Melville's vision of life does not admit of neat and simplified categories of destruction and creation, of life and death. If we recognise this, we will discover no incompatibility in identifying Vishnu and Moby Dick; for we cannot really say that one is a preserver, and the other, a destroyer. Melville is aware that Vishnu, the Preserver, does possess attributes of the Destroyer. He describes him as "dread Vishnoo" and in the same sentence calls him "divine Vishnoo." The same fusion of the opposite qualities is to be found in every one of his incarnations: he is tender and terrible and destroys to preserve. Similarly, Moby Dick, the Destroyer, is also not without creative qualities. Moby Dick, we all know, is a sperm whale. His value in commerce depends upon the fact that he is "the only creature from which that valuable substance, spermaceti, is obtained." "Spermaceti" may not actually be the seminal fluid, as the name suggests, but Melville considers it to be so and describes it as "the quickening humor." This fluid was not only used medically for rejuvenation, but also for lighting lamps on ships and in homes. Incidentally, Vishnu, who is supposed to have a thousand names, is called *Vishwaretah,* which means the semen of the universe. It is obvious that Melville intended Moby Dick to represent both the creative and destructive forces of life. . . .

The commingling of diverse mythical material turns whale-hunting into a symbolic quest for God and Truth by elevating the white whale to a cosmic symbol and by bringing into focus the entire history and prehistory of man's religious strivings, recreating imaginatively the mythological splendor and unity of the ancient world. James Baird rightly observes that "Moby Dick in his fullness becomes the whole of man's religious history."

Moby Dick Is an Allegory of Humanity's Struggle with God

William Braswell

In the following selection, William Braswell quotes a French critic who summarizes the plot of *Moby Dick* by saying that the "only reason Ahab tries to harpoon Moby Dick is that he cannot harpoon God." Braswell argues that Ahab's quest to kill the white whale is an allegory of man's quest for revenge on God. Braswell is the author of *Melville's Religious Thought*, a study of Melville's religious background and its influence on his writing.

In his essay on "Hawthorne and His Mosses," Melville said that "in this world of lies, Truth is forced to fly like a scared white doe in the woodlands; and only by cunning glimpses will she reveal herself, as in Shakespeare and other masters of the great Art of Telling the Truth,—even though it be covertly and by snatches." The various interpretations of *Moby-Dick* testify to the difficulty of discovering the precise meaning of the novel from the cunning glimpses of truth it allows. . . . The interpretation given here, which agrees with a number of others in the importance it attributes to certain passages, confines itself to what seems significant for the understanding of Melville's religious spirit at the time he wrote the novel.

To come at once to the central problem, the meaning of the allegorical conflict between Ahab and Moby Dick, Melville says explicitly what Moby Dick symbolizes for Ahab. Ever since the combat in which the white whale bit off one of Ahab's legs,

> Ahab had cherished a wild vindictiveness against the whale, all the more fell for that in his frantic morbidness he at last came to identify with him not only all his bodily woes, but all

From William Braswell, *Melville's Religious Thought.* Copyright 1943, Duke University Press, Durham, N.C. Reprinted with permission.

his intellectual and spiritual exasperations. The White Whale swam before him as the monomaniac incarnation of all those malicious agencies which some deep men feel eating in them, till they are left living on with half a heart and half a lung. That intangible malignity which has been from the beginning; to whose dominion even the modern Christians ascribe one-half of the worlds; which the ancient Ophites of the East reverenced in their statue devil;—Ahab did not fall down and worship it like them; but deliriously transferring its idea to the abhorred White Whale, he pitted himself, all mutilated, against it. All that most maddens and torments; all that stirs up the lees of things; all truth with malice in it; all that cracks the sinews and cakes the brain; all the subtle demonisms of life and thought; all evil, to crazy Ahab, were visibly personified, and made practically assailable in Moby-Dick. He piled upon the whale's white hump the sum of all the general rage and hate felt by his whole race from Adam down; and then, as if his chest had been a mortar, he burst his hot heart's shell upon it.

The novel also plainly says that the assault on Moby Dick signifies more than a mere assault on evil. For evil is but an effect, and Ahab is interested in the primary cause. Reasoning by analogy, in the manner of divines arguing for God's beneficence, Ahab concludes that if good is to be attributed to the omnipotent Deity, so must evil. When gazing one day at a calm sea beneath "a smiling sky," he exclaims: "Look! see yon albicore! who put it into him to chase and fang that flying fish? Where do murderers go, man? Who's to doom, when the judge himself is dragged to the bar?" For him the visible world is but the manifestation of the spiritual: ". . . not the smallest atom stirs or lives on matter, but has its cunning duplicate in mind." When Ahab strikes at Moby Dick, the symbol of all spiritual as well as all physical evil, he does so in a mad desire for revenge on God, whom he holds responsible for its existence. Ahab explains this when he says to Starbuck:

All visible objects, man, are but as pasteboard masks. But in each event—in the living act, the undoubted deed—there, some unknown but still reasoning thing puts forth the mouldings of its features from behind the unreasoning mask. If man will strike, strike through the mask! How can the prisoner reach outside except by thrusting through the wall? To me, the White Whale is that wall, shoved near to me. Sometimes I think there's naught beyond. But 'tis enough. He tasks me; he heaps me; I see in him outrageous strength, with an inscrutable malice sinewing it. That inscrutable thing is chiefly what I hate; and be the White Whale agent, or be the White Whale principal, I will wreak that hate upon him.

HARPOONING GOD

A contemporary French critic got at the heart of the matter when he said that the only reason Ahab tries to harpoon Moby Dick is that he cannot harpoon God.

By various devices Melville makes the white whale an imposing symbol of divine power. The crazy Shaker prophet Gabriel pronounces Moby Dick to be "no less a being than the Shaker God incarnated." Although Moby Dick is represented as an agent for the first cause rather than as the first cause itself, to conceive of a god's being incarnate in a whale

SUPERNATURAL REVENGE

In this excerpt from Moby Dick, *narrator Ishmael ponders Ahab's reasons for pursuing the white whale, coming to the conclusion that it is a monomaniacal hatred too deep to penetrate.*

Ahab had purposely sailed upon the present voyage with the one only and all-engrossing object of hunting the White Whale. Had any of his old acquaintances on shore but half dreamed of what was lurking in him then, how soon would their aghast and righteous souls have wrenched the ship from such a fiendish man! They were bent on profitable cruises, the profit to be counted down in dollars from the mint. He was intent on an audacious, immitigable, and supernatural revenge.

Here, then, was this grey-headed, ungodly old man, chasing with curses a Job's whale round the world, at the head of a crew, too, chiefly made up of mongrel renegades, and castaways, and cannibals—morally enfeebled also, by the incompetence of mere unaided virtue or right-mindedness in Starbuck, the invulnerable jollity of indifference and recklessness in Stubb, and the pervading mediocrity in Flask. Such a crew, so officered, seemed specially picked and packed by some infernal fatality to help him to his monomaniac revenge. How it was that they so aboundingly responded to the old man's ire—by what evil magic their souls were possessed, that at times his hate seemed almost theirs; the White Whale as much their insufferable foe as his; how all this came to be—what the White Whale was to them, or how to their unconscious understandings, also, in some dim, unsuspected way, he might have seemed the gliding great demon of the seas of life,—all this to explain, would be to dive deeper than Ishmael can go.

is not unprecedented, as Melville was aware. Twice in the novel he refers to the oriental myth of "the incarnation of Vishnu in the form of leviathan." And he plays with the idea of a leviathan deity by asserting that "If hereafter any highly cultured, poetical nation shall lure back to their birth-right, the merry May-day gods of old; and livingly enthrone them again in the now egotistical sky; in the now unhaunted hill; then be sure, exalted to Jove's high seat, the great sperm whale shall lord it." He suggestively compares the white whale with Jupiter incarnate in a white bull, and even refers to the whale as "the grand god."

Moby Dick is invested with "terrors unborrowed from anything that visibly appears," and with some attributes unmistakably divine. Haunted by the legends about him, superstitious sailors believe him to be both ubiquitous and immortal. His intelligence is considered far superior to mere animal instinct: ". . . such seemed the White Whale's infernal aforethought of ferocity, that every dismembering or death he caused, was not wholly regarded as having been inflicted by an unintelligent agent." There is a supernatural awe in his whiteness, which "is at once the most meaning symbol of spiritual things, nay, the very veil of the Christian's Deity; and yet . . . the intensifying agent in things the most appalling to mankind." At the end of the novel, just after the whale with "retribution, swift vengeance, eternal malice" in his aspect has rammed the ship, Ahab cries that the hull is "god-bullied.". . .

Since Ahab's attitude toward the Deity is precisely the opposite of Christlike submissiveness, it is ironically appropriate that the *Pequod* sets sail on Christmas Day. Ahab's incantation over the harpoon he tempers in savage blood is also in harmony with his defiance: "*Ego non baptizo te in nomine patris, sed in nomine diaboli.*" The omission of reference to the Son and the Holy Ghost emphasizes the fact that Ahab's feud is with God alone. As Ahab pursues the white whale, he continues venting his blasphemy, though in a veiled way. Since Melville was depending for his livelihood on the sale of his books in a Christian land, and since, moreover, he had no perverted desire to offend good Christian people, he caused Ahab to address his insulting remarks to "the gods," "the heavens," "thou clear spirit," and the like. What Ahab says makes it fitting that he should have been named after King Ahab of old, who, according to the Bible, "did more to provoke the Lord God of Israel to anger than all the kings of Israel that went before him." (He is like the scriptural Ahab also in that a prophetic Elijah foretells his doom.) . . .

FIRE AS SYMBOL

In another scene he calls the gods jacks-of-all-trades, and says that they are unprincipled. In the typhoon he becomes vulgar toward the Deity. "What a hooroosh aloft there!" he cries of the winds. "I would e'en take it for sublime, did I not know that the colic is a noisy malady. Oh, take medicine, take medicine!"

Some of Ahab's more serious charges against the Deity are made in the chapter entitled "The Candles," which tells how during the storm the corposants appeared: "All the yard-arms were tipped with a pallid fire; and touched at each tri-pointed lightning-rod-end with three tapering white flames, each of the three tall masts was silently burning in that sulphurous air, like three gigantic wax tapers before an altar." The symbolism implies what Melville goes on explicitly to say: "God's burning finger has been laid on the ship." Using fire as a symbol for the Deity might have been suggested to him by knowledge of Zoroastrianism, Heraclitus, the Stoics, the Bible, or various other sources.

Instead of being awed by this "Mene, Mene, Tekel Upharsin," Ahab defiantly brings charges against the Deity. One of them is suggestive of Gnostic influence. In primitive Christian times the Gnostics urged rebellion against the Creator of the universe. They taught that He is an emanation from a higher power, that He is ignorant of His genealogy, and that He tyrannically governs the world in the belief that He is the Supreme God. . . .

REASONS TO DEFY GOD

The most important comments that Ahab makes about God are those which give the reason for his defiance. By way of preface to the following quotation, Ahab's being burned in the act of worshiping fire, or God, on the high seas may be clarified by recalling that Melville uses exploring the seas to represent looking for the highest truth and that in *Pierre* he refers to fire as "an eloquent symbol" of the "ultimate Truth itself" (in *Moby-Dick* he says that "clear truth is a thing for salamander giants only to encounter"). Having fire symbolize both the Deity and the ultimate truth is not strange when one recalls the theological notion that God not only is true but is the Truth. As to Ahab's burn, he is described on his first appearance in the novel as bearing a long white scar like that which lightning sometimes makes in the trunk of a lofty tree. . . .

GOD IS WITHOUT LOVE

It is clear that Ahab conceives God to be without love for mankind. When Melville was completing *Moby-Dick*, he wrote to Hawthorne: "The reason the mass of men fear God, and *at bottom dislike* Him, is because they rather distrust His heart, and fancy Him all brain like a watch." Ahab typifies this dislike of God for His heartlessness. Looking upon the misery of the insane black boy Pip, Ahab exclaims: "There can be no hearts above the snow-line. Oh, ye frozen heavens! look down here. Ye did beget this luckless child, and have abandoned him, ye creative libertines." He says that Pip shall henceforth live with him, and Pip, clasping his hand, declares that he will never let go; whereupon Ahab cries: "Lo! ye believers in gods all goodness, and in man all ill, lo you! see the omniscient gods oblivious of suffering man; and man, though idiotic, and knowing not what he does, yet full of the sweet things of love and gratitude." Ahab's severity with his crew should not blind one to the fact that his pity for mankind motivates his hostility toward the Deity.

Ahab maintains that he is predestined to play the role that he plays. "This whole act's immutably decreed," he tells Starbuck. "'Twas rehearsed by thee and me a billion years before this ocean rolled. Fool! I am the Fates' lieutenant; I act under orders.". . .

ADMIRATION FOR AHAB

Though Melville makes it clear that Ahab is responsible for his doom, he also shows great admiration and sympathy for Ahab. Melville considered Hawthorne and himself men of great hearts and keen intellects. He represents Ahab as "a mighty pageant creature"—a man "with a globular brain and a ponderous heart." Some men do not have souls, but Ahab has enough "to make up for all deficiencies of that sort in other chaps"; to use his own bold figure, though his body has but one leg his "soul's a centipede, that moves upon a hundred legs." Possessed of keen perception, Ahab is unable to enjoy the common delights of men. His abnormal consciousness of the grief in the world has made him "impatient of all misery in others that is not mad.". . .

AHAB AS CHRIST

Ahab, one might say, has taken upon himself the suffering of mankind. In a way to remind one of Jesus Christ, he is pictured as standing before his men "with a crucifixion in his face; in all the nameless regal overbearing dignity of some mighty woe." The "Iron Crown of Lombardy" that he wears was made, as Geist observes, "of the nails used in the Crucifixion." Ahab feels as though he "were Adam, staggering beneath the piled centuries since Paradise." His attack on the evil symbolized by Moby Dick, together with this arraignment of God for permitting evil, is madly enacted in behalf of mankind. At the head of thirty-six foreigners, an "embassy of the human race," Anacharsis Clootz in 1790 spoke before the French Assembly for the rights of man. Melville refers to Ahab's crew as an "Anacharsis Clootz deputation from all the isles of the sea, and all the ends of the earth, accompanying Old Ahab in the *Pequod* to lay the world's grievances before that bar from which not many of them ever come back." Most men, like Stubb, laughingly refuse to think about the problem of evil; or, if they do think about it, solve it, like Starbuck, by letting "faith oust fact." If Ahab were not intellectually honest and courageous, if he were less affected by the suffering of mankind, he would not be the tragic figure he is. As it is, too much reflection on the problem of evil brings him to madness. . . .

MOBY-DICK AND MELVILLE'S ATTITUDES

Melville does not try to refute Ahab's criticism of the Deity as hardhearted. He does not say that God is loving and merciful. On the contrary, *Moby-Dick* contains evidence apart from what Ahab says that Melville thought of God as not wholly benevolent. The rhetorical apostrophe to "the great democratic God" is notable of Melville's democracy rather than of his adoration for a benevolent Deity. On the same page he says that "at the undraped spectacle of a valour-ruined man" piety itself cannot "completely stifle her upbraidings against the permitting stars": the thought behind the astrological figure is obvious. . . .

We have Melville's own testimony on the spirit in which he wrote the novel. During the final stages of work on it he declared in a letter to Hawthorne:

> Shall I send you a fin of the *Whale* by way of a specimen mouthful? The tail is not yet cooked, though the hell-fire in which the whole book is broiled might not unreasonably have cooked it ere this. This is the book's motto (the secret one), *Ego non baptiso te in nomine*—but make out the rest yourself.

We know from Ahab's incantation over his harpoon that the secret motto in full is: "*Ego non baptizo te in nomine patris, sed in nomine diaboli.*" In the letter Melville does not say that this is Ahab's motto; he says that it is the book's. And in a letter to Hawthorne just after *Moby-Dick* was published, Melville says: "I have written a wicked book, and feel spotless as the lamb." He does not say a book with a wicked character in it; he says a wicked book. And of course it was a wicked book according to the Christian world in which Melville and Hawthorne lived. Melville's inability to account for evil had made him conclude that the Christian conception of a wholly benevolent Deity is wrong, and he had arrived at the point where he could give full artistic expression to his heretical view without suffering pangs of conscience. Considering how far he had come from his early orthodox position, and how also the everlasting years of Carlyle, Emerson, and a host of others were ringing in his ears, there was reason for him to feel somewhat self-conscious, even though he was writing to a friend whom he believed to be, like himself, a thunderer of no.

Moby Dick Is an Allegory About the Unconscious

D.H. Lawrence

Novelist D.H. Lawrence is best known for his work *Lady Chatterley's Lover*, which caused a scandal when it was published in 1928 because of its sexually explicit content. Lawrence was greatly influenced by psychologists Sigmund Freud and Carl Jung, whose work focused on unconscious motivations for people's conscious acts. In this article, Lawrence argues that *Moby Dick* is an allegory of man's last mythological hunt, which ends with his becoming one with his environment.

Herman Melville's biggest book is *Moby Dick*, or *The White Whale*. It is the story of the last hunt. The last hunt, the last conquest—what is it?

American art symbolises the destruction, decomposition, mechanizing of the fallen degrees of consciousness.... [James Fenimore] Cooper and Melville [show] the deeper worship-through-contumely of the fallen sexual or sacral consciousness; [Edgar Allan] Poe the direct decomposition of this consciousness; and [Richard Henry] Dana and Melville the final hunting of the same consciousness into the very Matter, the very watery material, last home of its existence, and its extinction there. Remains the entry into the last state, and into fulness, freedom.

St. John said, "there shall be no more sea." That was esoteric. Exoterically, Dana and Melville say the same. The Sea, the great Waters, is the material home of the deep sacral-sexual consciousness. To the very depths of this home Melville pursues the native consciousness in himself, and destroys it here. When he has really destroyed this sacral-sexual consciousness, destroyed or over-thrown it, then

From *The Symbolic Meaning: The Uncollected Versions of "Studies in Classic American Literature"* by D.H. Lawrence, edited by Armin Arnold (New York: Viking; Fontwell, U.K.: Centaur Press, 1962). Reprinted by permission of Centaur Press.

John's prophecy will be fulfilled. There will be no more sea.

Moby Dick is the story of this last symbolic hunt. Moby Dick is a great white whale, the Leviathan of the waters. He is old, hoary, monstrous and snow-white; unspeakably terrible in his wrath; having been repeatedly attacked, he swims now alone in the great, pathless seas.

He is the last warm-blooded tenant of the waters, the greatest and last. He is the deep, free sacral consciousness in man. He must be subdued.

In himself he is warm-blooded, even lovable. But he must be conquered. Curious are his counterparts in the world. The whole of the South Pacific seems to worship, in hate, the shark or the crocodile, the great cold-blooded tenants, lords of the water, fiendish and destructive lords. Curious how shark and crocodile patterns, with grinning teeth, dominate aboriginal decoration-designs in those regions. The same crocodile worship is found in Africa, very widespread. In China, however, the dragon, the Leviathan is the dragon of the sun: as the Mantis, surely another dragon of the sun, dominates the Bushmen. Is not this the inordinately ancient relic of the pre-Flood worship, a relic from that era when the upper consciousness was the anathema [thing despised], and the glory and the triumph was all in the sensual understanding, incomprehensible to us now?

Melville writes in the peculiar, lurid, glamorous style which is natural to the great Americans. It gives us at first a sense of spuriousness. To some it merely seems wordy and meaningless, unreal. It comes, I think, from the violence native to the American Continent, where force is more powerful than consciousness, and so is never gracefully expressed. The life-force itself is so strong that it tends to come forth lurid and clumsy, obscure also. It causes also a savage desire to go to extremes, to hasten to extremes, whether of idealism or of violent action.

STRUCTURE

So, in beginning *Moby Dick*, we must be prepared for the curious lurid style, almost spurious, almost journalism, and yet *not* spurious: on the verge of falsity, still real. The book starts off with a semi-metaphysical effusion about water, and about the author's attraction to this element; it goes on with some clumsy humorisms, till it arrives in the sea-town of New Bedford. Then actual experience begins. It is curiously like cold material record, touched-up into journalese: neither veritable nor created. One cannot help feeling that the author is pretentious, and an amateur, wordy and shoddy. Yet something glimmers through all this: a glimmer of genuine reality. Not a reality of real, open-air experience. Yet it is a reality of what takes place in the dark cellars of a man's soul, what the psychoanalysts call the unconscious. There is the old double set of values: the ostensible Melville, a sort of Emersonian transcendentalist, and the underneath Melville, a sort of strange underworld, under-sea Yankee creature looking with curious, lurid vision on the upper world. It is the incongruous mixture of ideal heaven and the uncouth incoherence of a self-conscious adolescent. The reality comes from the adolescent, the uncouth, unformed creature, not from the idealist.

It is no use pretending that Melville writes like a straight-forward, whole human being. He is hardly a human being at all. He gives events in the light of their extreme reality: mechanical, material, a semi-incoherent dream-rendering. What the futurists have tried hard to do, Dana and Melville have pretty well succeeded in doing for them. These two are masters of the sheer movement of substance in its own paths, free from all human postulation or control. The result is nearly like artifice, a sort of rank journalism. But we must restrain a too hasty judgment. The author is never quite himself. He is always at the mercy of the rank, self-conscious idealism which still rules white America, he always has to handle artificial values.

Melville tries to square himself with the intellectual world by dragging in deliberate transcendentalism, deliberate symbols and "deeper meanings." All this is insufferably clumsy and in clownish bad taste: self-conscious and amateurish to a degree, the worst side of American behavior. When however he forgets all audience, and renders us his sheer apprehension of the world, he is wonderful, his book commands a stillness in the soul, an awe.

Let us repeat that it is in rendering the sheer naked slidings of the elements, and the curious mechanical cause-and-effect of materials [sic] events, that he is a master. For near as he is to sheer materialism, the central creative spark is still unquenched, the integral soul is present, if alone. His mind lags far, far behind his physical comprehension. His mind is cumbered up with the hopeless aggregation of fixed ideas, which spin on together like little wheels. But his bodily knowledge moves naked, a living quick among the stark elements. In sheer physical, vibrational sensitiveness, like a marvelous wireless-station, he registers the effects of the outer world. And he records also, almost beyond pain or pleasure, the extreme transitions of the isolated, far-driven soul, the soul which is now alone, without human connection.

CHAPTER 4

Billy Budd

Billy Budd Is a Tale of Acceptance

William Ellery Sedgwick

In the following selection, William Ellery Sedgwick claims that even though *Billy Budd* is a tragedy, the character of Billy is meant to offset this tragedy. Sedgwick believes that Billy's innocence, goodness, and natural charisma prove that human goodness compensates for all of the tragic, senseless evil in the world. Sedgwick authored the book *Herman Melville: The Tragedy of Mind*, from which this article is excerpted.

It is right and true to call *Billy Budd* Melville's "testament of acceptance"; but we must be careful not to understand either too much or too little by the word acceptance. Melville's "acceptance" was not based on any denial of the tragic facts of life or any ignorance of the inexorable logic of these facts. The world which we are shown in his last book is figuratively—as he had called it long before in *White-Jacket*—and literally, a man-of-war world, and the story of *Billy Budd* is as stark a tragedy as an American writer even to this day has ever penned.

The scene is an English man-of-war, the *Indomitable*, near the close of the eighteenth century, when conservative England and revolutionary France were locked in mortal combat. The hero, a young English sailor, is hanged for an act which his superiors, bound by the articles of war, have to adjudge a crime for which hanging was the only commensurate punishment, but which, in reality, far from being evil, was like the swift retributive stroke of an indignant angel.

Billy is the handsome sailor—guileless, good-natured, loving and beloved. Opposite him, like the bad angel against the good angel in an old morality, is the ship's police officer or master-of-arms, John Claggart. Out of apparently motive-

From *Herman Melville: The Tragedy of Mind* by William Ellery Sedgwick (Cambridge, MA: Harvard University Press, 1944). Copyright 1944 by the President and Fellows of Harvard College. Reprinted by permission of the publisher.

less malice, Claggart is down on Billy and trumps up a charge against him. In the captain's cabin, in the presence of the captain, he accuses Billy of trying to incite the crew to mutiny. Now Billy has one deformity; he stammers. Bewildered and outraged, he cannot find the words to defend himself and repel Claggart's accusation. His whole being rises, and, since words fail him, he takes other means to express himself. Quick as a flash and with the force of a cannon shot, he drives his right fist at Claggart's jaw and floors him. A few moments later the ship's surgeon pronounces the master-at-arms dead. "It is the divine judgment of Ananias," Captain Vere exclaims to the astonished surgeon; but again starting, he vehemently exclaimed, "Struck dead by an angel of God. Yet the angel must hang." From this point on the interest centers in Captain Vere as he faces the dilemma which flashed upon him in these words.

Of the captain's character something more should be told. He is an excellent officer; there are few better than he in His Majesty's service. While always mindful of the welfare of his men, he will not tolerate any infraction of discipline. . . .

VERE

Being the man he is in the position he occupies, Captain Vere acts promptly in the emergency which has taken place before his eyes. He immediately summons his lieutenants to sit in court martial on Billy Budd. Captain Vere's directions to his court martial cannot be overlooked. They bring out a point of special urgency as they also show his character in action. Of Claggart's inexplicable malice, which provoked Billy to strike him, the captain says, "Ay, there is a mystery; but to use a Scriptural phrase, it is 'a mystery of iniquity'; a matter for psychological theologians to discuss. But what has a military court to do with it?" Nor is the question of Billy's intent or non-intent pertinent. "The prisoner's deed, with that alone we have to do." Neither the speculative mind nor the heart has any business here; "the heart is the feminine in man and hard though it be, she must here be ruled out." Captain Vere understands the compunctions that his fellow officers must feel, and he reviews them; "In natural justice is nothing but the prisoner's overt act to be considered? Now can we adjudge to summary and shameful death a fellow-creature innocent before God and whom we feel to be so?— Does that state it aright? You sign sad assent. Well, I too feel

that, the full force of that. It is Nature. But do these buttons
that we wear attest that our allegiance is to Nature? No, to the
King. Though the ocean, which is inviolate Nature primeval,
though this be the element where we move and have our

ENVY

*From the moment he first spies Billy, Claggart tries to undo
him. In this excerpt from* Billy Budd, *the narrator speculates
as to why Claggart is so envious of Billy. Melville's comparison of Claggart to a snake, and therefore a sort of Satan figure, is evident.*

Now envy and antipathy, passions irreconcilable in reason, nevertheless in fact may spring conjoined like Chang
and Eng in one birth. Is Envy then such a monster? Well,
though many an arraigned mortal has in hopes of mitigated
penalty pleaded guilty to horrible actions, did ever anybody
seriously confess to envy? Something there is in it univer-
sally felt to be more shameful than even felonious crime.
And not only does everybody disown it, but the better sort
are inclined to incredulity when it is in earnest imputed to
an intelligent man. But since its lodgment is in the heart not
the brain, no degree of intellect supplies a guarantee against
it. But Claggart's was no vulgar form of the passion. Nor, as
directed toward Billy Budd, did it partake of that streak of
apprehensive jealousy that marred Saul's visage perturbedly
brooding on the comely young David. Claggart's envy struck
deeper. If askance he eyed the good looks, cheery health,
and frank enjoyment of young life in Billy Budd, it was because these went along with a nature that, as Claggart mag-
netically felt, had in its simplicity never willed malice or experienced the reactionary bite of that serpent. To him, the
spirit lodged within Billy, and looking out from his welkin
eyes as from windows, that ineffability it was which made
the dimple in his dyed cheek, suppled his joints, and danc-
ing in his yellow curls made him pre-eminently the Handsome Sailor. One person excepted, the master-at-arms was
perhaps the only man in the ship intellectually capable of
adequately appreciating the moral phenomenon presented
in Billy Budd. And the insight but intensified his passion,
which assuming various secret forms within him, at times
assumed that of cynic disdain, disdain of innocence—to be
nothing more than innocent! Yet in an aesthetic way he saw
the charm of it, the courageous free-and-easy temper of it,
and fain would have shared it, but he despaired of it.

being as sailors, yet as the King's officers lies our duty in a sphere correspondingly natural?" No, for "in receiving our commissions we in the most important regards ceased to be natural free agents. When war is declared, are we the commissioned fighters previously consulted? We fight at command.... So now, would it be so much we ourselves that would condemn as it would be martial law operating through us? For that law and the rigor of it, we are not responsible. Our vowed responsibility is in this: that however pitilessly that law may operate, we nevertheless adhere to it and administer it. ... But while, put to it by those anxieties in you which I cannot but respect, I only repeat myself—while thus strangely we prolong proceedings which should be summary, the enemy may be sighted and an engagement result. We must do; and one of two things must we do—condemn or let go."

Captain Vere reminds the court of the larger situation which they must keep in mind. Their country is at war with another power; conservative England is threatened from without and from within. The sparks from the French Revolution have crossed the Channel. Mutinies have flared up in the English navy—there has been the mutiny at the Nore, the so-called Great Mutiny—and, although quelled, these outbreaks might be repeated at any moment. Hence, more than ever, His Majesty's officers are bound to insist on all points of discipline. A clement sentence in the case of Billy Budd might be construed as timidity and encourage insurrection. Says Captain Vere, turning the case over to his subordinates, "You see then whither, prompted by duty and the law, I steadfastly drive. But I beseech you, my friends, do not take me amiss."

The other officers "hardly had the inclination to gainsay one whom they felt to be an earnest man, one, too, not less their superior in mind than in naval rank." Billy is convicted and sentenced to hanging at the yard arm in the early morning watch, it now being night. The next morning, just at daybreak, the sentence was carried out. ...

NATURE AND THE WORLD

Of all the ship's company only Captain Vere and Claggart were "intellectually capable of adequately appreciating the moral phenomenon presented in Billy Budd." As for Claggart, as Captain Vere had the insight to discern, in him there was the opposite mystery to Billy's, "the mystery of iniquity." What, Melville asks, "can more partake of the mysterious than the antipathy spontaneous and profound such as is invoked in certain exceptional mortals by the mere aspect of some other mortal, however harmless he be?—if not called forth by that harmlessness itself." Normal human nature affords no explanation of such a one as Claggart, who is at once an object of pity and of the profoundest loathing. He and his kind are free of vulgar vices. He is, says Melville, borrowing a definition attributed to Plato, a case of "Natural Depravity; a depravity according to nature." Melville explains that this is not the same as Calvin's total depravity, because it does not apply to all mankind, but only to certain individuals. This much Melville has to say about the origin of evil. But his interest in his last book is not primarily speculative or metaphysical. It is enough for him that the mysterious facts are confronted—are confronted honestly and honorably.

Melville distinguishes between nature and the world. Primeval nature is good. The world is not under nature's rule. Not nature, not love, but necessity, or fate, rules the world. It is a man-of-war's world and we all fight at command. Idealism which would throw off this yoke of necessity only leads to more misery for man. Of the last decade of the eighteenth century, when the story takes place, Melville wrote, "The opening proposition made by the Spirit of that Age involved the rectification of the Old World's hereditary wrongs. In France, to some extent, this was bloodily effected. But what then? Straightway the Revolution itself became a wrongdoer, one more oppressive than the kings. Under Napoleon it enthroned upstart kings, and initiated that prolonged agony of continual war whose final throe was Waterloo." However unintelligible and arbitrary, there is an organic necessity in the world and it cannot be disregarded. A principle of limitation, it is, nevertheless, also a principle of self-preservation. Even where it allows some latitude for choice, men are wise to conform with it by supplementing it with forms and definitions of their own. Captain Vere only repeats Melville's own, now settled conviction, "With mankind . . . forms, measured forms, are everything; and that is the import couched in the story of Orpheus with his lyre spellbinding the wild denizens of the woods." And "this he once applied to the disruption of forms going on across the Channel and the consequences thereof.". . .

VERE'S SOUL

As an index to Melville's "acceptance," Captain Vere is still more interesting as he faces his own soul. He is obliged by the exigencies of this man-of-war world to disregard all considerations of the absolute good and the ultimate truth. But he does not therefore deny the existence of the absolute good and the ultimate truth. He is the first to recognize Billy's angelic innocence. In the present emergency his innocence cannot excuse the consequences of his act: "We proceed under the law of the Mutiny Act." But he has said, "At the Last Assizes it shall acquit." In his dilemma Captain Vere does not arraign God as a devil-god; nor does he conclude, according to *Pierre*, "that whatever other worlds God may be Lord of, he is not the Lord of this." The words occur in the Plinlimmon pamphlet, and in *Pierre* Melville could not bring himself to accept Plinlimmon's relativistic doctrine of virtue in this world. Like his hero, he would have all or nothing and, like his hero, he got nothing; or, because his imagination could not picture nothing, he got worse than nothing: "Now, 'tis merely hell in both worlds."

As Plinlimmon wrote, "What man who carries a heavenly soul in him, has not groaned to perceive, that unless he committed a sort of suicide as to the practical things of this world, he can never hope to regulate his earthly conduct by the same heavenly soul? And yet by an infallible instinct he knows, that that monitor cannot be wrong in itself." So it was with Captain Vere. As for Melville, it can be said that he has accepted the human predicament,—which follows inevitably from the dualism of human nature. . . . Now he sees that because a man acts under a worldly necessity he does not therefore debase his humanity: his soul, be it immortal or not, is not soiled thereby. And because a man has accepted the limitations of his nature he is not therefore lacking in human strength and dignity, and is not to be relegated, as we feel that Melville, in the presence of Ahab could not but relegate Starbuck, on the score of "the incompetence of mere unaided virtue or right-mindedness." Further than this he sees that it is possible to be in this world and not of it; that because a man has taken on the burden of human consciousness, with its sad knowledge of good and evil, he is not therefore excommunicated from primal goodness.

Between Billy's instinctive rectitude, that of an upright barbarian, and such as Adam's might have been "ere the urbane Serpent wriggled himself into his company," and Captain Vere's conscious human rectitude there is no estrangement. Far from that, there is a profound reciprocal understanding between the two.

> Fair encounter
> Of two most rare affections! Heavens rain grace
> On that which breeds between them!

It was Captain Vere who, of his own motion, communicated the death sentence to Billy. As to what transpired then, between these two, "each radically sharing in the rarer qualities of one nature," Melville would no more than hint. Captain Vere was old enough to have been Billy's father. "The austere devotee of military duty, letting himself melt back into what remains primeval in our formalized humanity, may in the end have caught Billy to his heart, even as Abraham may have caught young Isaac on the brink of resolutely offering him up in obedience to the exacting behest. But there is no telling the sacrament . . . wherever under circumstances at all akin to those here attempted to be set forth—two of great Nature's nobler order embrace." The next morning when Billy stood up for execution before the crew, his last words were "God bless Captain Vere." Not long afterward Captain Vere, dying of a wound received in an engagement with the enemy, was heard to murmur words inexplicable to his attendant, "Billy Budd, Billy Budd."

It is possible to see in these intimations the reflection of a heavenly mystery, in which the idea of divine love, as attributed to Christ, is reconciled with the known facts of the rough justice which overrules the world. There is a suggestion of such a reconciliation in terms of Christianity inasmuch as it is just hinted that Billy Budd, a foundling, was in truth, the son of Captain Vere. It should be mentioned, too, since no fact in the story is without some symbolical significance, that the enemy's ship which Captain Vere engaged and overcame, at the cost of his life, formerly named the *St. Louis*, had, by the revolutionary government of France, been re-christened the *Athéiste*. Furthermore, it is impossible not to see in Billy's execution a resemblance to the Crucifixion. Long after his death, his comrades "recalled the fresh young image of the Handsome Sailor, that face never deformed by a sneer or subtler vile freak of the heart within! This impression of him was doubtless deepened by the fact that he was gone, and in a measure mysteriously gone." The spar from which he was hanged was reverently kept track of even long after it had been discarded. To those who had known Billy "a chip of it was as a piece of the Cross." At the moment of his death before the assembled crew, "it chanced that the vapory fleece hanging low in the east, was shot through with a soft glory as of the fleece of the Lamb of God seen in mystical vision, and simultaneously therewith, watched by the wedged mass of upturned faces, Billy ascended; and ascending, took the full rose of the dawn."

MAN'S NATURE IS GOOD

It may be that the visitations of man's best nature signify a more than human reality. It may be that such innocence and goodness as blazed in Billy's heart have a sanction from a higher quarter than the tribunals of this world. Melville does not say. "Doubts of all things earthly,"—that is, doubts of all earthly beliefs and conclusions,—and "intuitions of some things heavenly,"—that was Melville's state of mind in his last book; a state of suspended belief and unbelief, in which, as I quoted Keats as saying, there is no "irritable reaching after facts and reason."

For the rest, in the "testament of acceptance," Melville ascribes a constitutional soundness to humanity. Insofar as it was provoked by wilful idealists, the French Revolution led to worse oppression than before. But taking a long view of it and seeing it as an infection coming to a head in a frame so constitutionally sound as to be able to throw it off, it had a salutary effect which "not the wisest could have foreseen" at the time. In a way "analogous to the operation of the Revolution at large, the Great Mutiny, though by Englishmen naturally deemed monstrous at the time, doubtless gave the first latent prompting to most important reforms in the British navy." Moreover, there is that in the foreground of the story which attests the constitutional soundness of humanity. Between normal human nature and a being like Claggart there is a gap, a "deadly space between." The sailors instinctively distrust him and are repelled by him. Whereas to Billy they respond spontaneously. They are drawn together around him as around a bon fire on a cold day and are stirred to acts of good nature by his cordial influence. . . .

In Billy's life there is more promise of salvation for the world than there is of damnation in his death. And Melville has partaken of its salvation. His intellectual passion spent, and illuminated by his insight of a mind which by accepting its limitations has transcended them and has found within itself, at its own mysterious centre, a calm not to be found elsewhere, Melville has been restored to the radiant visage of life, whose shining secret is, it has its salvation in its own keeping.

Billy Budd Is a Rebel

John Bernstein

John Bernstein graduated from Princeton University and is a professor of English at Macalester College in St. Paul, Minnesota. In the following selection, Bernstein argues that Melville intended *Billy Budd* as a story of rebellion against the constraints of society. Although Bernstein contends that Melville implicitly criticizes both Vere and Billy, Melville finds rebellion a route preferable to following society's arbitrary rules.

"That's rebellion," murmured Alyosha, looking down. "Rebellion? I am sorry you call it that," said Ivan earnestly. "One can hardly live in rebellion, and I want to live. Tell me yourself, I challenge you—answer. Imagine that you are creating a fabric of human destiny with the object of making men happy in the end, giving them peace and rest at last, but that it was essential and inevitable to torture to death only one tiny creature—that baby beating its breast with its fist, for instance—and to found that edifice upon its unavenged tears, would you consent to be the architect on those conditions? Tell me, and tell the truth." "No, I wouldn't consent," said Alyosha softly.

Dostoyevsky, *The Brothers Karamazov*

In *Billy Budd* Melville ... condemns not only Claggart, but Captain Vere and perhaps even Billy as well, and that though the work is strongly anti-war, the ultimate message, first stated in the Preface, is a call to rebellion, not only philosophical rebellion but violent revolution if necessary.

The seeds for the tragedy of *Billy Budd* are sown when the hero is seized aboard the merchant ship, the *Right-of-Man*, and impressed into service on the British warship, the H.M.S. *Indomitable*. Billy's transfer represents more than a mere change of scenery, for the differences between the two ships are the differences between two worlds with conflicting sets of values, and the young sailor is destroyed because

From *Pacifism and Rebellion in the Writings of Herman Melville* by John Bernstein (The Hague: Mouton, 1964). Reprinted by permission of the author.

he is unable to adjust to the more complex and sinister life on the *Indomitable.*

The *Rights-of-Man,* as the name indicates, is a place in which the rights of every individual are respected. It symbolizes at once an unfallen world in which inherent evil does not exist, and also a primitive world, such as the Valley of the Typees, where man is governed not by a codified set of laws, but by natural law. Billy, who "in the nude might have posed for a statue of young Adam before the Fall" and who is "a sort of upright barbarian, much such perhaps as Adam presumably might have been ere the urbane serpent wriggled himself into his company," is eminently suited for life aboard such a ship as the *Rights-of-Man.* Because of his physical beauty and moral purity, Billy emerges as a natural leader among the crew of this vessel. "Ashore he was the champion; afloat the spokesman; on every suitable occasion always foremost." And, as Captain Graveling remarks to Lieutenant Ratcliffe, the officer who impresses young Budd, Billy is the peacemaker aboard the *Rights-of-Man.*

The world represented by the H.M.S. *Indomitable* is antithetical to Billy's former ship. To begin with, the *Indomitable* is not a vessel of commerce but a ship of war, and as such, is subjected to much the same sort of condemnation as is the *Neversink* in *White-Jacket. . . .* Life on the merchant vessel was governed by the rights of man. Aboard the *Indomitable,* the Articles of War, which have no concern with right or wrong but merely with expediency and which are highly arbitrary, prevail. Under these Articles, the individual has few rights, as Billy's impressment demonstrates, and man is regarded not as a free and thinking being, but merely as a pawn of the King's.

GOOD VERSUS EVIL

Most important of all, however, there exists a type of evil on the warship which was lacking aboard the *Rights-of-Man.* This is embodied in Claggart, the Master-at-Arms, "in whom was the mania of an evil nature, not engendered by vicious training or corrupting books or licentious living, but born with him and innate, in short, 'a depravity according to nature.'" As we have seen, Billy is described as being similar to Adam before the Fall. This Biblical imagery is further developed by Claggart, who assumes the role of the Serpent in the Garden of Eden. (The Master-at-Arms looks at Billy with "serpent fascination," and when Billy and Captain Vere attempt to lift Claggart's corpse, "it was like handling a dead snake."

The Adam-like Billy is an easy victim for the serpent-like Claggart. The young man is so innocent and naive that he is unable to perceive evil, much less to cope with it. Billy's dilemma is instantly recognized by the aged Dansker, who speculates "as to what might eventually befall a nature like that, dropped into a world not without some man-traps and against whose subtleties courage lacking experience and address without any touch of defensive ugliness, is of little avail." When small things start going wrong for Billy— something awry with his hammock or the storage of his gear—he appeals to the oracular Dansker for advice. The old man comments that "*Jemmy Legs*" (a nickname for Claggart), is down on him. Such sinister subtlety completely eludes the young sailor. "'*Jemmy Legs!*' ejaculated Billy his welkin eyes expanding; 'what for? Why he calls me *the sweet and pleasant young fellow*, they tell me.'"

But *Jemmy Legs* is indeed down on Billy, so much so that the Master-at-Arms concocts an elaborate plot and accuses young Budd of planning mutiny. This is a particularly serious charge in the year 1797, the time in which the story is set, for England is not only at war with France, but the British Navy has been rocked with a series of mutinies. When Captain Vere hears this accusation, he summons Billy to his cabin in order for the youth to hear Claggart's charges face to face. Now Billy has one flaw in his otherwise flawless make-up: he stutters. When Claggart repeats his slander, Captain Vere urges Billy to speak in his own defense. But Billy, unable to protect himself in the face of evil, cannot speak. Captain Vere, realizing the problem, tells Billy to take as much time to reply as he needs. But the usually pacifistic Billy still can't utter a word. "The next instant, quick as the flame from a discharged cannon at night, his right arm shot out, and Claggart dropped to the deck." After Captain Vere affirms that the Master-at-Arms has been killed by this blow, he exclaims "'Struck dead by an angel of God. Yet the angel must hang.'"

This rapid evaluation by the *Indomitable*'s captain not only neatly summarizes the basic tension of *Billy Budd*, but sheds a great deal of light on the character of Vere himself. What kind of a man is this who can so quickly size up a situation and so quickly pass judgment? . . .

Captain Vere is a wise man, "mindful of the welfare of his men, but never tolerating an infraction of discipline." Vere's wisdom springs from three sources—from his own personal experience, from his vast reading ("books treating of actual men and events no matter what era—history, biography, and unconventional writers, who, free from cant and convention, like Montaigne, honestly and in the spirit of common sense philosophize upon realities.") . . .

Vere's wisdom is coupled with goodness. Throughout Billy's ordeal, he shows a consummate kindness to the young sailor, so much so, that, during the trial when Billy becomes confused, he turns "an appealing glance towards Captain Vere as deeming him his best friend and helper." After Billy has been sentenced, Vere makes an unprecedented visit to the compartment of the condemned foretopman, and exists from this interview in a greater state of suffering than the prisoner himself. . . . Despite Captain Vere's kindly and paternal feelings towards Billy (Melville likens the older man's attitude toward the condemned youth to Abraham's compassion for Isaac), he nevertheless believes that the young seaman must hang, for since the British Navy is not only involved in a war, but threatened by rebellion from within, to allow the killing of an officer to go unpunished would encourage mutiny among the British sailors and might eventually lead to an overthrow of the entire English system. Moreover, such punishment must be immediate. Thus Vere's sense of duty wins out over his sense of compassion, and he argues to the hastily summoned drumhead court that Billy must be sentenced to death. Chronometrical law must be ignored if the law of man is to survive, as Vere attempts to make clear to the confused and unphilosophical members of the court. . . .

VERE'S DECISION IS EVIL

Though compassionate and kindly as Vere may be, though his plea for Billy's execution is honest, painful, and carefully thought out, the Captain advocates an evil and wrong verdict. Melville is no more able to accept a system founded upon the sacrifice of an innocent babe than is Ivan Karamazov, the intellectual hero of Dostoyevsky's monumental novel *The Brothers Karamazov*, a work which deals with virtually the same theme as does *Billy Budd* and which comes to somewhat the same conclusions. If a system can exist

"FATED BOY"

In this excerpt from Billy Budd, *Captain Vere demands that Billy answer Claggart's accusations against him. Because of his stutter, Billy ends up killing Claggart. Many of the main themes in* Billy Budd *are revealed here, including Melville's likening of Billy to Christ.*

"Speak, man!" said Captain Vere to the transfixed one, struck by his aspect even more than by Claggart's. "Speak! Defend yourself!". . .

Though at the time Captain Vere was quite ignorant of Billy's liability to vocal impediment, he now immediately divined it, since vividly Billy's aspect recalled to him that of a bright young schoolmate of his whom he had once seen struck by much the same startling impotence in the act of eagerly rising in the class to be foremost in response to a testing question put to it by the master. Going close up to the young sailor, and laying a soothing hand on his shoulder, he said, "There is no hurry, my boy. Take your time, take your time." Contrary to the effect intended, these words so fatherly in tone, doubtless touching Billy's heart to the quick, prompted yet more violent efforts at utterance—efforts soon ending for the time in confirming the paralysis, and bringing to his face an expression which was as a crucifixion to behold. The next instant, quick as the flame from a discharged cannon at night, his right arm shot out, and Claggart dropped to the deck. Whether intentionally or but owing to the young athlete's superior height, the blow had taken effect full upon the forehead, so shapely and intellectual-looking a feature in the master-at-arms; so that the body fell over lengthwise, like a heavy plant tilted from erectness. A gasp or two, and he lay motionless.

"Fated boy," breathed Captain Vere in tone so low as to be almost a whisper, "what have you done! But here, help me."

The twain raised the felled one from the loins up into a sitting position. The spare form flexibly acquiesced, but inertly. It was like handling a dead snake.

only if its most innocent and just members must be sacrificed, then this system is not worth preserving. Though white civilized man might be appalled at the conclusion that it is better for an innocent man to be spared and society to collapse completely with all the resulting anarchy than it is for society and its institutions to be preserved at the cost of one of its members, this is nonetheless the direction towards which Melville is inexorably pointing in *Billy Budd.*

Though there is no criticism of Vere's integrity, his decision as to the necessity of sacrificing Billy to preserve the law is sharply attacked by Melville. When the Surgeon is summoned into Vere's cabin to ascertain whether Claggart is dead, something in the Captain's attitude makes him wonder if Vere's mind has suddenly become affected. The Surgeon's doubts are echoed and re-echoed in the succeeding pages. "Whether Captain Vere, as the Surgeon professionally and primarily surmised, was really the sudden victim of any degree of aberration, one must determine for himself by such light as the narrative may afford." Even Vere's fellow officers question his wisdom in these proceedings. "Certain it is however that subsequently in the confidential talk of more than one or two gun-rooms and cabins he was not a little criticized by some officers." Nevertheless, it must be emphasized—as the Captain himself stresses—that Vere is acting not through his own volition but as an agent of martial law. The fact that Vere is such a good man makes it even more clear that the responsibility for Billy's death lies with such arbitrary codes as the Articles of War and the Mutiny Act rather than with any specific individual.

I have earlier suggested that Melville takes not only Captain Vere to task, but Billy Budd as well. Moreover, in his criticism of Billy, we find perhaps Melville's most subtle attack on Christ. There is little doubt that by the end of the novel, Billy has acquired Christ-like characteristics. Claggart's accusations bring to Billy's face "an expression which was as a crucifixion to behold." At the moment that Billy is hanged,

> it chanced that the vapory fleece hanging low in the East, was shot through with a soft glory as of the fleece of the Lamb of God seen in mystical vision and simultaneously therewith, watched by the wedged mass of upturned faces, Billy ascended, and ascending, took the full rose of the dawn.

After Billy's execution, the spar from which he was hanged was in great demand among common sailors, for "To them a chip of it was as a piece of the Cross."

BILLY'S WAY IS INEFFECTIVE   .

As we have seen, Billy was a natural leader aboard the *Rights-of-Man,* a peacemaker and a spokesman among the crew. In an unfallen world, Billy is a tower of nobility and strength, a righter of wrongs. But in a fallen world, a world of innate evil and Claggarts, the philosophy represented by Billy is ineffective. This is indicated immediately when Billy is impressed by Lieutenant Ratcliffe. The Handsome Sailor does not resist this injustice, he seems almost to welcome it. "To the surprise of the ship's company, though much to the Lieutenant's satisfaction, Billy made no demur.... Noting this uncomplaining acquiescence, all but cheerful one might say, the shipmates turned a surprised glance of silent reproach at the sailor." When Billy is questioned by the drumhead court as to whether he would participate in a mutiny, he replies, "'I have eaten the King's bread and I am true to the King.'" This answer indicates that Billy seems completely unaware that not only he, but a large part of the crew which has also been impressed, are unquestionably the victims of injustice, and that the King is ultimately one of the chief sources of this injustice. When shortly before his execution Billy calls out "God bless Captain Vere!" and this shout is echoed by the crew, Billy in one sense is again furthering the system of injustice which has doomed him and others. It is one thing to bless Captain Vere as an individual, and it is another thing to accept so quietly the decisions of the inherently evil authority invested in Captain Vere. In his calm acceptance of what befalls him and others, Billy himself becomes an unconscious tool of injustice, for he is a natural leader, yet he does nothing to help free the mass of mankind from their fetters. Billy's life—as is Billy's death—is meaningless and wasteful, and offers not hope to mankind, but despair. In the character of Billy Budd, whose "smooth face all but feminine in purity" recalls descriptions in the author's earlier writings about the feminine nature of Christ, Melville is making his final and most profound observation on the character of Jesus and the nature of Christianity. To be Christ-like in a Christ-like and unfallen world is well and good. But a Jesus-like meekness in a fallen world does nothing to rectify the evil that exists therein. A more vigorous attitude is necessary if injustice is to be crushed out.

AN APPEAL TO REVOLUTION

The ultimate message of *Billy Budd* is an appeal to revolution, and the work is Melville's most complete statement on rebellion, both political and spiritual. Though critics comment upon the marvelous craftsmanship of *Billy Budd*, most of them ignore the implications of the Preface of the novel, which indicate the course of the action to follow and suggest the moral to be drawn.

> The year 1797, the year of this narrative, belongs to a period which as every thinker now feels, involved a crisis for Christendom not exceeded by its undetermined momentousness at the time by any other era whereof there is record. *The opening proposition made by the Spirit of that Age, involved the rectification of the Old World's hereditary wrongs. In France to some extent this was bloodily effected. But what then? Straightway the Revolution itself became a wrongdoer, one more oppressive than the kings.* Under Napoleon it enthroned upstart kings, and initiated that prolonged agony of continual war whose final throe was Waterloo. *During those years not the wisest could have foreseen that the outcome of all would be what to some thinkers apparently it has turned out to be, a political advance along nearly the whole line for Europeans.*
>
> Now, as elsewhere hinted, it was something caught from the Revolutionary Spirit that at Spithead emboldened the man-of-war's men to rise against real abuses, long-standing ones, and afterwards at the Nore to make inordinate and aggressive demands, successful resistance to which was confirmed only when the ringleaders were hung for an admonitory spectacle to the anchored fleet. *Yet in a way analogous to the operation of the Revolution at large the Great Mutiny, though by Englishmen naturally deemed monstrous at the time, doubtless gave the first latent promptings to most important reforms in the British Navy.* [Italics my own.]

Thus, the Preface implies that though rebellions such as the French Revolution often initially result in confusion and wrongdoing, they eventually may lead to important reforms and political advancement.

The theme of rebellion is further developed throughout *Billy Budd*. There are continual references to such important leaders of the French Revolution as Anacharsis Cloots and General Murat. The owner of the *Rights-of-Man* "was a staunch admirer of Thomas Paine whose book in rejoinder to Burke's arraignment of the French Revolution had then been published for some time and had gone everywhere." Indeed, two entire sections of *Billy Budd* in addition to the Preface—Sections Three and Five—are devoted entirely to an analysis of revolution and mutiny.

Billy Budd, therefore, is a struggle between the forces of rebellion and those who are opposed to rebellion, such as Admiral Nelson, who is continually cited throughout the novel, and Captain Vere, a man who opposes revolutions not because he was a member of the aristocracy but because "they seemed to him incapable of embodiment in lasting institutions, but at war with the peace of the world and the true welfare of mankind." But the fate of Billy Budd, who is often likened to Adam and who on one level is representative of Everyman, condemns the system and the authority represented by men like Vere and Nelson. Such authority can only be effectively opposed by active rebellion. Captain Vere is eventually slain in a combat with the French ship, the *Athéiste*, whose name obviously symbolizes the forces of the French Revolution, which, as may be remembered, Melville suggests led to "a political advance along nearly the whole line for Europeans.". . .

Throughout the world, men are suppressed and victimized by systems of authority such as the Articles of War. Though good men such as Captain Vere often administer these codes, there can be no justice under a system which is inherently wrong. Nor can the cause of justice for all be furthered by a Christ-like resignation to the authorities who represent this system. Freedom and justice can be gained only by vigorously striking out against the offending system and its authorities. This rebellion, as evidenced by the French Revolution, may itself for a time become perverted and act as a tool of injustice. But in the long run, the force of rebellion, which is a combination of social and, in a sense, spiritual protest, is that power which eventually liberates mankind. . . .

MELVILLE'S PROTEST

In an age and a country which was, for the most part, content to ask orthodox questions and give orthodox answers, Melville dived deep into the meaning of existence and was not afraid to face the consequences of his findings. In all of his major works, we find an unflagging search for truth and a refusal to accept anything which might be considered unjust or shoddy. Moreover, there is as much idealism and defiance of conventional attitudes in his more mature work as in his earlier writings. Jay Leyda has noted that "Glued on the inside of the writing box on which *Billy Budd* and the last poems were composed was found a tiny clipping—Melville's own motto—'Keep true to the dreams of thy youth.'" Melville's intellectual wanderings led him to condemn God and to challenge the basis of Christianity. Though in this sense Melville might be considered the phenomenologist of relativism, he was an absolutist in his refusal to compromise his principles. For Melville, the universe was basically hostile to the human race, but like Albert Camus he felt that "there are more things to admire in man than to despise." And, what is perhaps the keynote to Melville as a writer and as a thinker, is his insistence that mankind is never more noble than in this struggle against injustice, both human and universal, that by rebelling against evil, man can wrest meaning from the cosmos and in this struggle find some sort of salvation.

CHRONOLOGY

1819

United States acquires Florida from Spain; Herman Melvill is born in New York City, the third child and second son of Allan Melvill (a merchant and son of a participant in the Boston Tea Party) and Maria Gansevoort (daughter of a revolutionary hero).

1820

National census: population 9,638,453; 7 percent urban, 93 percent rural.

1823–1825

Monroe Doctrine proclaimed; Herman attends New York Male High School but is not fond of books.

1826

Herman contracts scarlet fever.

1827

Herman visits grandparents in Boston.

1828

Herman is named best speaker in his school.

1829

Herman enrolls in the Grammar School of Columbia College.

1830

Father's business fails; Melvill family moves to Albany and Herman attends Albany Academy.

1831

Herman wins first prize in his class for bookkeeping.

1832

After father's death on January 28, Herman and brother Gansevoort are withdrawn from Albany Academy; Gansevoort opens a fur and cap store; Herman is put to work in his Uncle Peter's bank; cholera strikes Albany in summer; mother takes children to uncle Thomas's farm in Pittsfield, Massachusetts; sends Herman back at insistence of Uncle Peter.

1833

Andrew Jackson defeats John Quincy Adams for presidency; Gansevoort adds an *e* to family name.

1834

Herman works in bank; in summer he works in brother's fur and cap store.

1835

Herman enters the Albany Classical School; cousins Thomas W. Melvill and Leonard Gansevoort join crews of whaling ships.

1836

Republic of Texas formed; Herman starts classes at Albany Academy and joins the Ciceronian Debating Society.

1837

Gansevoort Melville's business fails; Herman attends winter term in a rural school near Pittsfield and teaches there until early 1838.

1838

Family moves to Lansingburgh, New York; Herman enrolls in Lansingburgh Academy to study surveying and engineering.

1839

Herman's first known fiction, "Fragments from a Writing Desk," appears in a Lansingburgh paper; signs on a merchant ship to Liverpool as a "boy"; in winter, teaches school near Greenbush, New York.

1840

On December 31 in New Bedford, Massachusetts, Herman signs on the whaling ship *Acushnet* for a voyage to the South Seas.

1842

First message by Morse's telegraph; Herman deserts ship with a companion in the Marquesas Islands and lives with the Typee tribe; Herman is crippled by a leg injury and friend Toby goes for help; Herman rescued by the crew of the whaler *Lucy Ann*; Herman takes part in another rebellion and is imprisoned in Tahiti for several weeks; signs on as a harpooner and boatsteerer to the *Charles & Henry* to go to Japanese whaling grounds.

1843

Melville is discharged in the Hawaiian Islands, works in Honolulu as a pin setter in a bowling alley and as a store clerk; signs on the U.S. Navy frigate *United States*.

1844

Melville discharged from navy in Boston; visits family; writes out his adventures with the Typee tribe.

1845

Gansevoort takes the manuscript of *Typee* with him to London to place with a publisher.

1846–1848

United States engages in Mexican-American War.

1846

Typee published.

1847

Omoo published; Melville marries Elizabeth Shaw in August and moves into a house in New York City with brother Allan and wife and Maria Melville and her four unmarried daughters; Melville joins the literary circle of Evert A. Duyckinck.

1848

Women's Rights Convention at Seneca, New York; Melville begins work on *Mardi*.

1849

The Melvilles' first child, Malcolm, is born; *Mardi* published; Melville writes *Redburn* and *White-Jacket*; *Redburn* published; Melville sails to London to arrange publication of *White-Jacket*.

1850

Melville returns to United States; begins writing *Moby Dick*; meets Nathaniel Hawthorne and buys a farm near Pittsfield; *White-Jacket* published.

1851

Melville manages to work on *Moby Dick* in between planting crops; in October second child, Stanwix, is born; *Moby Dick* published in October under the title *The Whale*.

1852

Melville gets into financial trouble; *Pierre*, published in July, receives terrible reviews and permanently damages his reputation in the United States; since the book is not published in England, his career remains somewhat less tarnished there.

1853

Melville writes *The Isle of the Cross*, but it is not published, forcing him to write a series of short tales to make money; "Bartleby the Scrivener" published; all income from Harper's, American publisher of his books, ends after a fire destroys stock of his books; Elizabeth (Lizzie), third child and first daughter, is born.

1854

Melville begins serializing *Israel Potter*; Putnam's publishes "The Encantadas."

1855

Fourth child, daughter Frances, is born.

1856

The Piazza Tales published; father-in-law funds a vacation for Melville, who sails to Glasgow and visits Hawthorne in Liverpool; continues on to the Mediterranean and Palestine.

1857

Melville goes to Egypt, the Holy Land, Greece, Sicily, Naples, and Rome; *The Confidence-Man* published in London and New York on or around April Fool's Day; Melville continues to tour northern Italy, Switzerland, Germany, and the Netherlands, returning to England and then home in May; begins to lecture on "Statues in Rome."

1860

Abraham Lincoln elected president; Melville sails for Cape Horn and San Francisco on a ship commanded by youngest brother, Thomas; returns in November.

1861–1865

American Civil War.

1861

Father-in-law dies.

1863

Melville sells Pittsfield farm to his brother Allan and moves with family to New York.

1864

Melville visits a cousin serving in the Army of the Potomac.

1865

Lee surrenders at Appomattox Courthouse; Lincoln assassinated.

1866

Battle-Pieces and Aspects of the War published; Melville receives a job as a customs inspector in New York.

1867

Melville's oldest son, Malcolm, shoots himself; Lizzie waits all day for Malcolm to get up, till Melville returns from work, forces open the door, and finds Malcolm dead in his bed.

1870–1875

Melville continues to write poetry, completing the eighteen-thousand-line *Clarel.*

1874

First Impressionist exhibit in Paris.

1876–1877

Clarel published in June; Melville works on several short fictional pieces.

1879

Edison invents workable incandescent lightbulb.

1882

Indian chief Geronimo captured; Plains Indian warfare ends; Melville's first grandchild, Eleanor, is born to Frances.

1885

French chemist Louis Pasteur gives first inoculation against rabies; Melville writes "Billy in the Darbies," receives an inheritance, and resigns from the customhouse.

1886

Melville's second son, Stanwix, dies; Melville works on *Billy Budd.*

1888

John Marr and Other Sailors, with Some Sea-Pieces published in September.

1891

Timoleon and Other Ventures in Minor Verse published in June; Melville suffers a fatal heart attack; *Billy Budd* left incomplete at his death.

WORKS BY HERMAN MELVILLE

Typee: A Peep at Polynesian Life During a Four Months' Residence in a Valley of the Marquesas (1846)

Omoo: A Narrative of Adventures in the South Seas (1847)

Mardi: And a Voyage Thither (1849)

Redburn: His First Voyage (1849)

White-Jacket; or, The World in a Man of War (1850)

Moby Dick; or, The Whale (1851)

Pierre; or, The Ambiguities (1852)

Israel Potter; His Fifty Years of Exile (1855)

The Piazza Tales (1856) (Contains "Bartleby the Scrivener," "Benito Cereno," "The Lightning-Rod Man," "The Encantadas," "The Bell-Tower," "The Piazza")

The Confidence-Man: His Masquerade (1857)

Battle-Pieces and Aspects of War (1866)

Clarel: A Poem and Pilgrimage in the Holy Land (1876)

John Marr and Other Sailors, with Some Sea-Pieces (1888)

Timoleon and Other Ventures in Minor Verse (1891)

POSTHUMOUS PUBLICATIONS

Billy Budd (1924)

Jack Gentian Sketches (1924)

Collections of shorter tales, sketches, first published in magazines

FOR FURTHER RESEARCH

BIOGRAPHIES

Gay Wilson Allen, *Melville and His World.* New York: Viking Press, 1971.

Charles Roberts Anderson, *Melville in the South Seas.* New York: Dover Publications, 1966.

Alice Kenney, *The Gansevoorts of Albany: Dutch Patricians in the Upper Hudson Valley.* Syracuse, NY: Syracuse University Press, 1969.

Herman Melville, *Melville's Journal of a Visit to London and the Continent, 1849–1850.* Eleanor Melville Metcalf, ed. Cambridge, MA: Harvard University Press, 1948.

Eleanor Melville Metcalf, *Herman Melville: Cycle and Epicycle.* Cambridge, MA: Harvard University Press, 1953.

Charles Olson, *Call Me Ishmael.* San Francisco: City Lights Books, 1947.

Raymond M. Weaver, *Herman Melville: Mariner and Mystic.* New York: Pageant Books, 1961.

Robert Wernick, "In Melville's Lifetime, Fame Proved Fickle," *Smithsonian,* July 1995, pp. 100–12.

CRITICISM

James Baird, *Ishmael.* Baltimore: Johns Hopkins University Press, 1956.

William Braswell, "Melville as a Critic of Emerson," *American Literature,* vol. 7 (1950), pp. 283–89.

Ray B. Browne, *Melville's Drive to Humanism.* Lafayette, IN: Purdue University Studies, 1971.

John Bryant, ed., *A Companion to Melville Studies.* Westport, CT: Greenwood Press, 1986.

William B. Dillingham, *An Artist in the Rigging: The Early Work of Herman Melville.* Athens: University of Georgia Press, 1972.

James Duban, *Major Fiction: Politics, Theology, and Imagination.* Dekalb: Northern Illinois University Press, 1983.

H. Bruce Franklin, *The Wake of the Gods.* Stanford, CA: Stanford University Press, 1963.

John Freeman, *Herman Melville.* New York: Haskell House Publishers, 1974.

Brian Higgins and Hershel Parker, eds., *Herman Melville: The Contemporary Reviews.* Cambridge, MA: Cambridge University Press, 1995.

Carolyn Karcher, *Shadow over the Promised Land: Slavery, Race, and Violence in Melville's America.* Baton Rouge: Louisiana State University Press, 1980.

A. Robert Lee, *Reassessments.* London: Vision Press, 1984.

Jane Mushabac, *Melville's Humor.* Hamden, CT: Archon Books, 1981.

Hershel Parker, ed., *The Recognition of Herman Melville: Selected Criticism Since 1846.* Ann Arbor: University of Michigan Press, 1967.

Faith Pullin, *New Perspectives on Melville.* Kent, OH: Kent State University Press, 1978.

John Samson, *White Lies: Melville's Narratives of Facts.* Ithaca, NY: Cornell University Press, 1989.

Merton M. Sealts Jr., *Pursuing Melville, 1940–1980.* Madison: University of Wisconsin Press, 1982.

Neal L. Tolchin, *Mourning, Gender, and Creativity in the Art of Herman Melville.* New Haven, CT: Yale University Press, 1988.

HISTORICAL OR LITERARY BACKGROUND

Ralph H. Gabriel, *The Course of American Democratic Thought.* New York: Ronald Press, 1940.

Daniel Walker Howe, ed., *Victorian America.* Philadelphia: University of Pennsylvania Press, 1976.

John P. McWilliams, *Hawthorne, Melville, and the American Character: A Looking Glass Business.* New York: Cambridge University Press, 1984.

Russel B. Nye, *Society and Culture in America, 1830–1860.* New York: Harper & Row, 1974.

Perry Miller, *The Raven and the Whale: The War of Words and Wits in the Era of Poe and Melville.* New York: Harcourt, Brace, 1956.

Edmundo O'Gorman, *The Invention of America.* Bloomington: Indiana University Press, 1961.

Richardson Wright, *Hawkers and Walkers in Early America.* Philadelphia: Lippincott, 1927.

INDEX